D1028885

The Literature of Cinema

ADVISORY EDITOR: **MARTIN S. DWORKIN**
INSTITUTE OF PHILOSOPHY AND POLITICS OF EDUCATION
TEACHER'S COLLEGE, COLUMBIA UNIVERSITY

THE LITERATURE OF CINEMA presents a comprehensive selection from the multitude of writings about cinema, rediscovering materials on its origins, history, theoretical principles and techniques, aesthetics, economics, and effects on societies and individuals. Included are works of inherent, lasting merit and others of primarily historical significance. These provide essential resources for serious study and critical enjoyment of the "magic shadows" that became one of the decisive cultural forces of modern times.

SOVIET CINEMA

Thorold Dickinson

and

Catherine De la Roche

ARNO PRESS & THE NEW YORK TIMES

NEW YORK • 1972

Publisher's Note: Catherine de la Roche has informed us that her text on the sound film was delivered early in 1947, having been written in the light of information available in London up to that time. Post-war difficulties delayed publication, by which time it had become apparent that some of the later events, such as the 1946 controversy, may have been misinterpreted by her.

Reprint Edition 1972 by Arno Press Inc.

Reprinted from a copy in The University of
  Illinois Library
LC# 77-169327
ISBN 0-405-03891-7

The Literature of Cinema - Series II
ISBN for complete set: 0-405-03887-9
See last pages of this volume for titles.

Manufactured in the United States of America

SOVIET CINEMA

SOVIET CINEMA

CINEMA

Thorold Dickinson

and

Catherine De la Roche

LONDON

THE FALCON PRESS LTD

First published in 1948
by The Falcon Press (London) Limited
7 Crown Passage, Pall Mall, London S.W. 1
Printed in Holland
by N.V. Drukkery Vada, Wageningen

CONTENTS

INTRODUCTION

For a quarter of a century the Soviet cinema has been one of the most vital and significant of the forces in modern culture, both from the social and the artistic standpoints. There has never been an adequate study of its achievement published in Britain since the days when the first excitement of seeing what are now called the silent classics of the middle and late 'twenties led to much enthusiastic appreciation being written some fifteen to twenty years ago. The present study in two essays has been undertaken by two different critics. The first essay deals with the period of the Soviet silent film, and shows its importance in that perspective which distance in time has now made more possible. The second essay, covering the Soviet sound film from its origins to the present day, offers both a record of what has been produced and an evaluation of the principles behind the later developments in the Soviet cinema. It should be emphasised, however, that this book does not attempt to be a complete and comprehensive history of the Russian film. It is rather an attempt to assess some of the more important elements in its contribution to the art of the cinema.

It is easy to overlook the fact that many of the most important Soviet films have never been either publicly or privately shown in this country, and that judgment based solely on the more obvious films which have been generally seen in Britain can be neither accurate nor just. Both of the critics responsible for this survey have been students of the Russian cinema for many years. Thorold Dickinson, himself a distinguished director of British films, has undertaken film research in many parts of the world and visited Russia before the war for the British Association of Ciné Technicians in order to study the developments taking place there. He was also a prominent official and later an active member of the Council of the London Film Society, which from its inception in 1925 was responsible for bringing many of the more significant Soviet films into Britain for private exhibition. Catherine de la Roche is of Russian origin, speaks the language fluently and has been for some time film critic to the only British journal published in the Soviet Union, *British Ally*. During the war she was Films Officer to the Soviet Relations Division of the Ministry of Information, and previously she had also the advantage of some years' experience in scenario work in the British film industry. She also played a leading part in the only

Russian-speaking dramatic society to function in Britain before the war.

No volume requiring the research which this study represents could have been made without the indispensable assistance of a number of organisations. We wish especially to thank *Soviet News* and The Society for Cultural Relations with Russia; the files of the first and the library of the second form part of the background from which our information came. The National Film Library of the British Film Institute gave invaluable assistance both in supplying sources of information and in making a large selection of stills from the silent films in their possession, and the splendid resources of the stills library of the Soviet Film Agency have supplied most of the unique collection of hitherto unpublished photographs which appear in this volume. We have deliberately given more space to examples from the lesser known Soviet cinema than to that already illustrated in other books previously published in this country. Without the assistance of all these organisations and the courtesy of their officials this volume could not have been published.

We have undertaken this work in the hope that the story it tells will make one aspect of Russian culture more intelligible to British people. We believe that the mutual recognition of the artistic achievements of different countries leads ultimately to a more vital understanding in other fields. It is with this hope in mind that we dedicate our book to our colleagues working in Soviet film production and film criticism.

ROGER MANVELL

The British Film Academy
London, 1948

THE SILENT FILM
IN RUSSIA

by

Thorold Dickinson

Before 1917

RUSSIA IS ONE of the few countries that do not claim to have made any contribution to the invention of the cinema. Stimulated by the success of their first film performance in Paris on December 28th, 1895, the Brothers Lumière, inventors of the cinema in France, sent showmen on tour through the continent of Europe to demonstrate their new discovery. Two of them brought the cinema to European Russia in 1898. To increase the attractiveness of their programmes, they made newsreels of easily accessible events in Russia itself and included them among their films, none of which occupied more than three or four minutes in the showing. The interest aroused provoked the newly founded French companies of Pathé and Gaumont to open branches for film distribution in Russia.

The firm of Pathé pioneered story film production there with *Tales of the Don*, which took six minutes to show. The first film studio began production in 1908 in a small building in Moscow, which later housed the Scientific Research Institute of the Film and Photo Industry of the RSFSR,[1] chief republic of the Soviet Union. Moscow became and remained the centre of the Russian film trade and industry and was responsible for ninety per cent of native production. The remaining ten per cent came from one small studio in the capital city of Petrograd, one in Kiev (opened in 1915), two in Odessa (opened in 1916), and two in Yalta in the Crimea, which were used as branch establishments by the leading Moscow producers, Ermoliev and Khanzhonkov. Ermoliev's output averaged as many as forty-eight films in the year. By 1917 twenty-two other producers had come into being, the best known being Neptune Films, Kharitonov and Company, and The *Russ* (or Russia) Company, which, reorganised, was to play a big part in production under the Soviet

---

[1] The Russian Soviet Federative Socialist Republic, which includes the greater part of European Russia, omitting the Ukraine, and part of Siberia.

regime. No film apparatus of any kind and no negative or positive film stock was manufactured in Russia. All technical equipment was imported, cameras from France and electrical gear from Germany.

The majority of films shown in Russia were also imported. More than seventy houses of distribution (a ludicrously high figure) catered for the one thousand and forty-five cinemas in the Russian Empire. Eighteen of these 'middle men' firms operated from Moscow, fifteen from Petrograd and over forty from other towns. As the average seating capacity of each cinema was three hundred and forty, amounting to less than one cinema for every hundred thousand of the population, the influence of the new medium could not have been formidable in this sixth part of the world.

The cinema was not yet the art form of the common man. Financially, and geographically outside the principal towns, it was to remain beyond his reach for several years to come. It would not have been economic to increase the seating accommodation in a country where the monthly wage of the worker averaged twenty rubles (or two pounds sterling at contemporary values) and where the peasant earned even less. And where seventy per cent of the population between the ages of eight and fifty were illiterate, the interpretation of screen captions would have been a problem. (Similar conditions prevailed in India in 1947, but there the talking film is an asset against eighty per cent illiteracy.)

In addition to these handicaps the development of the cinema was hampered by the conservative taste of the ruling class. Ballet and opera were the diversions of the aristocracy and the well-to-do, and progress in these arts was not tolerated. Hence the voluntary exile of Diaghilev and his ballet company in their determination to experiment.

Probably the most progressive productions of this period were the early puppet films which Ladislas Starevitch made for Khanzhonkov and the experiments made in 1915 and 1916 by Vsevolod Mayerkhold, the most advanced of Russian stage producers. For this period Mayerkhold left the theatre and produced as films 'The Picture of Dorian Gray' by Oscar Wilde, Ostrovsky's play 'The Storm' and Pshibuishevsky's 'The Strong Man'. These experiences influenced his return to the stage, for he built a film projector into the auditorium of his theatre and used film as an element in his stage productions. Thus Eisenstein as a student under Mayerkhold first came into working contact with the cinema.

Most Russian film production derived from stage plays and stories, romantic, sombre and often exotic. Comedies were rare. The general standard was mediocre. The most successful directors were Buchovetsky, Granovsky, Protazanov, Tourjansky, Volkov and the actor Ivan Moszoukin, whose output as player and director was prolific, particularly after

1914 when import of foreign films almost ceased owing to difficulties of war transport. Other players who became celebrated were Nikolai Kolin, Nikolai Rimsky, Natalie Kovanko, Natalie Lissenko and Xenia Desni. All these artists of the Russian cinema were to emigrate after the revolution, and of them Protazanov alone returned when working and living conditions began to become tolerable.

The centre of the Imperial Government was at Petrograd, and there operated the Scobelev Committee, which had charge of the production and distribution of government films for war propaganda, including a small number of motor vans equipped with single film projectors. While the products of the commercial industry were escapist and often pessimistic, those of the Scobelev Committee were directly aimed at discouraging the growing discontent among the civilian workers and the armed forces. But the scope of the committee was small and its work had no real force.

People do not revolt until they are convinced that no other state can be worse than their present condition. The times were corrupt, the dictatorial regime was heading for disaster. The fighting forces were badly equipped and underfed. Their home leave was infrequent. New troops arrived unarmed at the front line and could only defend themselves by stripping the dead of rifles and ammunition. Deserters left the front in hordes and poured back into the towns and villages where prices were high and food and fuel difficult to come by. Everywhere morale was low, for only a few understood and approved of the cause for which they were fighting. The cinema was used mainly to divert the minds of the wealthy from the cares of the masses. In this negative way it may have hastened the coming of the revolution.

1917 and after

The first revolution of March 1917 overthrew the czarist regime and gave power to a Provisional Government of liberal tendencies under the mild leadership of Kerensky, who tried to reorganise the state on democratic lines and to continue the war against Germany at the same time. One of the first acts of this new government was to stimulate film production by abolishing the strict censorship maintained by their autocratic predecessors. This popular gesture encouraged the production of entertainment films until by the end of the year over two-thirds of the films exhibited were of Russian origin and less than one-third were foreign.

The Provisional Government also reorganised the Scobelev Committee to produce two anti-czarist propaganda films, *Nicolas II* and *The Past will not Return,* which were largely made from material reassembled from existing films. These two pictures were not delivered until some weeks after the Bolshevik revolution of November 1917, and their effect on the members of the Petrograd Soviet may well be imagined. The Soviet Government decided that the more recent past should not return either. They scrapped the films, dismissed the liberal Scobelev Committee and replaced it with the Cinema Committee under the new Minister of Education, the playwright Lunacharsky.

The new Committee at once made two decisions. They put into production the first fictional propaganda film, *Congestion*, from an original scenario by Lunacharsky; the story told how a bourgeois family were won over to the revolution by the persuasive efforts of a working-class family, who had been moved from unhealthy tenements and billeted on the bourgeois household. The Committee's second decision was to open in Petrograd a school for training film actors and technicians, thus founding a movement which was to provide a steady flow of talent into the industry beyond the present day. Towards the end of 1918 a similar school was founded in Moscow. From 1918 onwards working conditions in the Petrograd studio were appalling. Worn-out equipment (four lamps doing the job of forty), shortage of food, fuel and transport physically handicapped the workers. Cameramen could allow themselves only one 'take' or performance of any shot, using in their cameras the 'short ends' of old rolls of unexposed negative, which were sometimes reduced to less than twenty seconds of running time. In the winter the thermometer indoors registered the equivalent of twenty degrees Fahrenheit.

A high proportion of the available unexposed film was used for making newsreels of the events of the revolution. Shortage of electric power closed all but forty-eight of Petrograd's three hundred cinemas. Projectors were stripped from the rest, mounted in motor vehicles and sent round the centres of the new Red Army in charge of lecturer-projectionists.

Early in 1918 when Petrograd came within range of German gunfire the Soviet Government moved to Moscow, which they made the capital of the republic. They decided to leave the Cinema Committee behind since the situation in Petrograd was much more favourable than in Moscow for the work of reorganising the film industry. In Petrograd the physical overthrow of the Kerensky Government had been short and sharp. In Moscow bloody street and house-to-house fighting had gone on for many days and had caused much damage and disruption. In Petrograd there were few counter-revolutionary elements in film circles, most of which consisted of the staffs of the cinemas. In Moscow where there were half the number of cinemas and much more production and distribution, the revolution caused the majority of the employers and intel-

12

lectuals in the industry to range their two associations—the OKO and The Tenth Muse, as they were called—against the new union of film workers which was in whole-hearted support of the Soviet regime.

Producers were more willing to collaborate with the new government than distributors or exhibitors, for the latter wanted to continue dealing in films completed under the former political system now in disfavour, while the producers were willing to bend their new subjects to the political line and so conserve their wealth and ensure its increase in circulation. Ermoliev, for instance, tried his hand at organising a propaganda film called *Andrei Koszhoukov,* directed by Protazanov and starring Moszhoukin, but this proved to be anti-czarist without being pro-Bolshevik. Political disfavour and the acute shortage of film stocks, new supplies of which were in any case withheld from those deemed to be politically unworthy of its use, led to Ermoliev closing down his activities in Moscow. Making his way south he crossed over into counter-revolutionary territory to continue work in his studio at Yalta in the Crimea. He was accompanied by most of the artists who were under contract to him, some of whom are named in the previous chapter.

The Crimea was occupied by counter-revolutionary forces until 1920, when in face of the approaching Red Army, Ermoliev with his human, cinematographic and literary assets emigrated to Paris to found the firm of Albatros Films.[1]

Possibly the greatest loss to the Soviet Cinema was Ladislas Starevich, who emigrated to Paris and there made further brilliant puppet films. In some of these the human figure appeared in conjunction with puppets for the first time together with the earliest known use of the backprojection process. Starevich had a light, satirical touch which in those days was almost unique among Russian film-makers.

These émigrés turned their backs on one of the grimmest episodes in modern history. With the end of the first world war in November 1918, the combatants on both sides reshuffled their positions and jointly invaded the Soviet territories on all frontiers a year after the Bolshevik revolution. The counter-revolutionary war of foreign intervention developing its full force in turn provoked an epidemic of typhus, which was followed by a food famine, both rendered more disastrous by the foreign blockade which prevented the import of medical supplies and foodstuffs. Financial chaos followed the collapse of the war and the withdrawal of the foreign interventionists and their Russian supporters in 1920. Tena-

---

[1] As late as 1925 the Billancourt studios (then under the control of Abel Glance) in the south-west of Paris were almost wholly staffed by Russian émigrés, some of whom had not yet troubled to learn more than a few words of French. High up on the wall of the main studio nearest the entrance was fixed an ikon of the Greek Orthodox Church. A noticeably large proportion of 'evening dress' film extras in Paris were Russian émigrés of high birth.

13

ciously the 200,000 members of the Communist Party under the leadership of Lenin clung to the power over 160,000,000 souls which they had assumed three years earlier. Those three years of struggle cost Russia over seven million lives and untold hardship for most of those who survived. This winter of 1920 was the most hellish time of all, when cold, hunger and disease weakened the stamina of even the stoutest supporters of the revolution.

Early in 1921 a serious naval mutiny at Kronstadt and uprisings of peasants in Siberia, the Ukraine and elsewhere forced the Soviet Government at last to accept a temporary setback, which nearly every other government on earth prayed should become permanent. In 1921 the government decreed the New Economic Policy by which the socialist system of production for use was set aside, and the national economy returned to production for profit and the legalising of private enterprise. Capitalism smirked its way back into circulation for a while, flourishing hectically for about a year. But over the next few years the new order recovered its strength and, by steadily reintroducing government controls, it gradually choked private enterprise out of existence, this time for good.

During these years of trial, films could expect no high priority in the government programme in spite of Lenin's recognising that 'cinema is for us the most important of arts'. While it took some five years politically to stabilise the new regime (1918-1922), two more were to elapse before the machinery of the film industry was efficiently reorganised in the RSFSR.

Nationalisation versus private enterprise

In the first months of the revolution living conditions proved more and more irksome to the bourgeoisie in the towns, now ruled by the new locally elected Soviets of workers and peasants. The antagonism of the merchants increased as each new decree further limited the scope of private enterprise. Film distributors retaliated by withholding copies of films from any cinemas which the local Soviets took over.[1]

Lunacharsky, who in May 1918 had moved the Cinema Committee from Petrograd to Moscow in order to be close to the offices of the

---

[1] The Moscow film trade paper 'Kinogazette', in its issue of the first week of April 1918, printed the following statement: 'Mr. Soloviev, proprietor of the Furor Theatre at Alexandrov, in the district of Vladimir, has announced that the Soviet of Workers' and Soldiers' Deputies of Vladimir has requisitioned his theatre with its apparatus and all its effects and is continuing to exploit it to their own profit, thus depriving its proprietor of his livelihood. Consequently the distributors' group begs the council of cinematograph organisations to instruct all distribution branch offices to discontinue all delivery of films to the Furor Theatre, Alexandrov.'

Government, realised that the only solution of the present anarchy was the complete nationalisation of the industry. This was accomplished in the RSFSR (and the republic of the Ukraine) in August 1919, not before many business men had managed either to hide their assets or to smuggle them out of the areas already in the hands of the Soviets.

This decree served to separate sharply the two schools of thought. It was preceded by signed petitions, bitter outcries in the film trade journals and anguished deputations of film stars, technicians of the higher grades and business men, who would not accept offers of permanent employment as adequate compensation for the loss of their physical assets and their private enterprise.

The few producers who accepted the new conditions found that their agreed programmes required an additional total of forty million feet of positive and negative film stock for their fulfilment. There was a delay of nearly two years before the war of intervention ended, the foreign blockade was raised and the trade agreements could be signed which provided for the renewal of imports and exports. Production and exhibition inevitably slowed down.

In 1921 with the re-introduction of private enterprise and the benefits of much-needed imports came more trouble for the Government. The business men who had gone into retirement rather than collaborate began to make hay while their private sun shone. But theirs was a tawdry triumph. Rather than let the new regime benefit from what they regarded as stolen property, they had allowed buildings and equipment to fall into disrepair. This happened everywhere except in Petrograd, where the workers kept the few cinemas still open in reasonable repair. Now that the new economic policy allowed them to return to private enterprise, the business men found that their cinemas, studios and film copies, which last had often been hidden, had fallen into a state of decay. By 1921 only five hundred and fifty out of 1,045 cinemas remained open or were able to reopen in the entire country. In Moscow ninety cinemas remained open out of one hundred and forty-three, and of these eighty reverted to private enterprise under their previous owners. In Petrograd, where we have already remarked a greater zeal for the revolution, only ten cinemas reverted to their previous owners out of the forty-eight which were still open. The remainder were managed co-operatively.

Private enterprise, almost unrestricted, led to financial inflation. Huntly Carter, who visited Moscow in 1922, quoted the case of a dramatic critic 'who has to live on slops at so many rubles a spoonful and to work till three in the morning at manual labour to pay for them'. Prices of seats in cinemas ranged from 500,000 to 2,000,000 rubles, cinema screens and upholstery were torn and dirty, buildings filthy and lousy, programmes lasted one hour or longer according to the number of times that the film broke.

Yet the Government noticed that even under these miserable conditions the customers poured in. The main source of attraction, it seems, was the renewed import of foreign films, which in turn stung the sorely tried studios in Russia to further and higher efforts. Films were indeed still being made, but emigration had created a genuine shortage of experts, and the new blood was not yet emerging from the training schools and the subordinate positions in which the newcomers were quite properly being grounded. Meanwhile there was a sad scarcity of imagination and polish in the creative and technical branches of film production.

Reconstruction of an industry

The removal of the Cinema Committee to Moscow in 1918 did not detract from the revolutionary enthusiasm of the film workers of Petrograd, who maintained their position as the political spearhead of the industry for several years to come. In their political fervour they completely ignored the susceptibilities of their colleagues in Moscow, whose work they judged to be inadequate in its attempts to express the new socialist ideas. Petrograd sent film units to Moscow to record important political events in the new capital city and to make and show films for medical and educational propaganda.

Moreover, when under the new economic policy of 1921 their film organisations were ordered to begin operating on a profit-making basis, the film workers of Petrograd adopted the new policy with equal ardour and efficiency, reorganising their central office co-operatively under the title of *Sevsapkino* and managing to run the foreign blockade and raise funds abroad with the help of the International Workers Aid organisation of Berlin. Through this channel they began to sell in 1921 in various countries of Europe and America two of their own productions — *Infinite Pity*, a story of the famine, and *The Miracle*, an episode from the reign of Nicholas I.

Then *Sevsapkino* had the temerity to transfer their main office of distribution to Moscow. They opened branches in Saratov, Rostov, Vitebsk and appointed an agent in Berlin. Through him they imported German and American films, including some of the work of Mary Pickford and Rudolph Valentino. Finally they began to acquire cinemas in Moscow itself.

This seemed to the Central Committee in Moscow to be carrying commerce too far. The theory of private enterprise was hateful enough, but here its competitive practice was beating the capitalists at their own game. It was evident that harmful, 'deviationary' tastes could be acquired just as much by compulsion as voluntarily. Petrograd·replied that the end justified the means. Making profits was secondary to their success in marketing socialist films in the rest of the world as well as in their own republics.

Moscow, however, won the debate by insisting that the benefits which *Sevsapkino's* own productions were conferring on their foreign audiences were being heavily outweighed by the reactionary tastes and tendencies expressed in the larger number of foreign films which they were importing and for which they were paying in Russian goods and Russian gold. These were the first practical signs in the cinema industry of the outcome of the Stalin-Trotsky argument. Hitherto Trotsky had managed to persuade his colleagues that socialism, to be permanent, could only thrive internationally.

Now Stalin was winning over communist opinion to his view that socialism could flourish in one country alone if it happened to be as large and as well endowed by nature as the Czarist Empire. The Soviet Union in his opinion could protect its socialism adequately from the antagonistic capitalist system of the outside world, without having first to convert foreign opinion to the Soviet system.

Other concerns than *Sevsapkino* were also showing foreign films to Russian audiences. Disturbed by the consequences of this private trading in bourgeois ideas, the Council of People's Commissars in December 1922 [1] decreed the reorganisation of the Cinema Committee and its ramifications into the *Goskino* or State Cinema Enterprise. The function of *Goskino* was to co-ordinate all the cinema activities of the RSFSR. This was the beginning of the end of the New Economic Policy (private enterprise) in the film industry. Each concern under the central authority had to continue to buy and sell in the commercial market, now hemmed in with increasing Government restrictions. All that *Goskino*, by its nature, was able to do was to interfere in the practices of a number of existing concerns and cause a great deal of friction in the process. For instance, *Goskino* forced *Sevsapkino* to draw in its horns and retire to its own home ground in the North-West Russian area where its operations were severely limited from their former scope.

To supply the ideological stimulus which had never sufficiently existed outside the Petrograd branch of the industry, the *Proletkino* (or proletarian cinema), a co-operative society, was founded by *Goskino* in April 1923. Petrograd inevitably resented the attempt to open a branch there, where indeed the aims of *Proletkino* had been efficiently executed

---

[1] At this same date the Union of Soviet Socialist Republics was formed, consisting at first of the Russian, the Ukrainian, the Transcaucasian and the Byelorussian Soviet Federative Socialist Republic.

from the earliest days of the revolution. But elsewhere *Proletkino* filled a strong political need in Russia and abroad by producing and supplying exclusively films which explored many aspects of the new Soviet point of view. *Proletkino* was to achieve all and more than all that *Sevsapkino* achieved in export without infecting the home market with imports which were politically suspect.

By the end of 1923 only 13 per cent of the films shown in Russia were of Soviet origin. Coming to the conclusion that the whole idea behind *Goskino* was unworkable because it did not go far enough, the Council of People's Commissars in 1923 set up a commission under one Mantzev to examine the present state of the industry and to make recommendations for its improvement. After several months of wrestling with the bureaucratic efforts of *Goskino* to straddle its unwieldy charge, the commission recommended that *Goskino* be superseded by a State Cinema Trust to control with state finance the entire cinema affairs of the Soviet Union. The Commissars found this suggestion too drastic and settled for a Trust with control in the RSFSR only.[1]

The decision was ratified in June 1924, and on March 1st, 1925, the celebrated *Sovkino Trust* came into being. Under the new constitution *Sevsapkino* retained its autonomy and changed its name to *Leningradkino*. One or two of the other staunch pioneer organisations were also allowed to retain their autonomy. Thus the organisational problems of the cinema in the largest Soviet republic were sorted out just at the time when the sorely needed first-fruits of the new schools of Soviet cinema production were beginning to reach the screen.

Among the other republics of the Soviet Union production had recommenced in 1921 in the Ukraine and had been begun for the first time by local initiative in Georgia and the Tartar Republic. The enthusiasm of the *Sevsapkino* organisation had also inspired the Soviets of Azerbaijan and Bukhara to ask Petrograd for help in founding film industries in their territories.

Production

It has been mentioned that *Sevsapkino* was allowed to retain its autonomy under the new centralised *Sovkino* concern. Another organisation that was deservedly awarded autonomy was the production and distribution group known by this time as *Mezhrabpom-Russ*, of Moscow. While *Sevsapkino* and its predecessors can be credited with keeping the newsreel and the factual film alive and of sufficiently good quality throughout the tribulations of the first seven years of revolution, their

[1] They did, however, make the Trust sole agent for film import and export to and from the entire Soviet Union.

18

work in fictional production could not of necessity remain constant or reach any reasonable standards of quality for lack of studio space and equipment.

The distinction of preserving continuity of studio production of quality belongs to the *Russ* (or Russia) Company which never closed down throughout this difficult period, adjusting itself to the changing conditions of revolution by turning itself into the Motion Picture Co-operative Society, Russia, of Moscow. The standard of production was sufficiently high during those early days to attract the collaboration of leading members of the Moscow Art Theatre and the theatres of Kameny and Mayerkhold.

The earliest Soviet production to be shown publicly in Great Britain was the most famous of the Russ productions of this period, *Polykushka*,[1] made in 1922 from a story by Leo Tolstoy, adapted by Fedor Ozep, directed by Sanin and starring I. M. Moskvin, a leading member of the Moscow Art Theatre. As Polykushka, the drunken serf who hangs himself after losing a sum of money entrusted to him by his owner, Moskvin gave a classic performance which is internationally memorable.

By 1922 the Russ studios were also producing children's films under the guidance of the Ministry of Education.

In 1923 the International Workers' Aid organisation of Berlin decided to extend its activities from relieving the physical needs of the Soviet peoples to influencing their minds through the film. They therefore bought a 90 per cent interest in the *Russ* concern, adding the truncated version of their name in Russian, *Mezhrabpom*, to the name of the old organisation.

Three of the new *Mezhrabpom-Russ* productions, of good quality and politically innocuous, were to be the next three Soviet films to be shown publicly in Great Britain: Pushkin's *The Postmaster* (starring Moskvin), *Morozko* (from the children's story *Father Winter*), both directed by Cheliabuzhsky, and Lunacharsky's *The Marriage of the Bear*, directed by Eggert. None of these films differed in style from the better class product of normal commercial studios elsewhere.

The most original Russian film in subject and design of this period was also made by this firm: Alexis Tolstoy's fantasy *Aelita*, set on Mars and in the Soviet Union in the years 1919-1920, which Protazanov returned from France to direct in 1924. Still photographs of the film

[1] First shown in Great Britain in 1924 at the St. James's Cinema, London (now the Westminster Theatre). A caption on the original version of the film described the production as having taken place in an unheated film studio during the severest winter on record. Food consisted of soup made from frozen potatoes.

19

reveal settings and costumes by Alexandra Exter which resemble the cubist style of some of the experimental work being done in the French cinema of the same period. The film penetrated as far as Central Europe, but like all the masterpieces of the remaining period of the Russian silent cinema it was too politically conscious for the British Board of (voluntary) Film Censors. Unlike these masterpieces, however, it was not imported into Great Britain for private exhibition. No written record of the film or comment on its quality extant is available. But it is said to have combined performances by players from both academic and experimental theatres and even from the circus. It would be interesting to meet someone who can recall having seen *Aelita*. Perhaps the film failed to fuse so many divergent styles of acting and of background. It is no encouragement for experiment that the articulate spectator makes no more concessions to a work which attempts the new than to one which expertly repeats the old.

The Russian cinema was now on the brink of the most vital period of innovation which the film industry of any nation has yet experienced. There were revolutionary ideas to illustrate, and the first batches of young technicians were evolving new ways to express them. The points of view involved in the reconstruction of the industry on a nationalised footing were no more conflicting than the theories which were competing to formulate the new techniques of production.

Manufacture of film projectors was begun in 1925 and increased the number of cinema installations from three thousand in 1926 to twenty-six thousand in 1934, playing to some five million seats. To feed this rapid increase of audiences newsreel production expanded, every event of significance being filmed, and cameras were sent to cover scientific expeditions and enterprises like the construction of the Turkestan-Siberian Railway, designed to link the granaries of Siberia with the cotton fields of Central Asia. Material of this kind was assembled into full-length 'chronicle' films. The *Turksib* film, directed by V. Turin for *Vostokkino*, production organisation for the autonomous republics in the east for the RSFSR, became internationally known as one of the most imaginative of silent factual films. It was notable for the successful handling of its main technical problem: it had to be completed before the railway itself was finished, and so its climax could not consist of the completion of the subject. Turin devised a climax which subsequently became a cliché, so often was it repeated in films elsewhere. He built a rapid recapitulation of the events already shown, lacing it up with an exciting arrangement of titles. The effect was powerful and satisfying.

Other types of films—scientific, educational and films for child audiences—began to supply the new cinema installations in hospitals, universities and training colleges, schools and children's institutes. Silent film production was to continue in the non-theatrical field long after the introduction of the sound film had reached the entertainment theatres.

In production for entertainment the right or artistically conservative wing of the movement was represented by the film directors of the theatrical school, who had survived the revolution and had remained in the service of the new regime; Chardynin, and Sanin and Gardin (of the *Russ* Co-operative) were the most prominent. Their artificial style of production and direction which had served to tide the industry over the formative years of the Soviet cinema now began to give way to the naturalistic style of the new centre group and to the style of cinematic realism of the left, progressive wing.

Directors of the straightforward, naturalistic school included two women: the former actress, Olga Preobrazhenskaya, whose *Peasant Women of Riazan* (1927) was a picturesque and sympathetic study of the changes in the position of women brought about by the Soviet Revolution, and Esther Shub, who specialised in reconstructions of episodes of recent history. In the Ukraine Stabavoi made a series of films, among them the sensational *Two Days* (1927), a tragedy of the disillusionment of an old caretaker who remained faithful too long to the old regime. Fedor Ozep made in *The Yellow Pass* (1927) an indictment of the czarist regulations regarding prostitution. Ozep was later to emigrate: in Berlin he directed a version of Tolstoy's play *The Living Corpse* (1929) with the film director Pudovkin playing the lead. Ozep did not return to the Soviet Union.

Probably the most imaginative exponent of the naturalistic school of direction was the Pole, Alexander Room. He made four silent films of which two gained international recognition: in 1927 *Triangle Love* (known abroad as *Bed and Sofa*), a frank comedy aimed at shocking male sexual complacency and the female acceptance of abortion, and *The Ghost that Never Returns* (1929), from the novel by Henri Barbusse. Room's style was simple, warm and intimate. To convey psychological conditions he used camera and editing unselfconsciously but imaginatively; the matter which he photographed was always realistic. To this day Room's work retains considerable vitality and freshness and bears comparison with much of the product of the progressive left wing who were making far and away the most significant Soviet contribution to the art of the cinema.

Dziga Vertov

The two pioneers of this group were the theorists, Lev Kuleshov and

21

the extremist, Dziga Vertov, innovator in the creative use of newsreel material. Vertov, a stocky, lively Ukrainian, was born in 1896 and was conscripted as a soldier in the first world war. Early in the civil war he became chief newsreel cameraman with the partisan army of Kozhevnikov. Then he began assembling his own films with such success that at the age of twenty-two he was made head of the cinema department of the All-Russian Central Executive Committee (of the RSFSR). At this early age he developed the theory which he was to pursue throughout his career, the theory of the camera as the film-eye. In 1919 he collected a number of fellow-enthusiasts into what he called the *Kinoki,* or Film-Eye, Group. In 1922 he began issuing a monthly newsfilm which he called *Film-Truth* and of which he completed twenty-three issues before beginning to work on full-length films.

Vertov was an austere fanatic who aimed at the recording of 'life caught unawares'. At first he allowed himself and his associates to stage nothing before the camera. None of his material was controlled except within the resources of the camera and the cutting room. The camera was, to him, a robot eye in the service of man. Scarcity of film stock and often the shortness of lengths of the negative film available taught him and his contemporaries the most rigid economy in the use of film. And this led them to turn this liability into an asset. Forced to join a series of short scenes together, they began first to fill in the gaps with sections of existing (even czarist) newreels. They found that the juxtaposition of certain scenes created conflict between the old material and the new. By this means they enriched their work with a new and dramatic style of cinema which had none of the literary or theatrical characteristics of the work of their contemporaries in fictional production.

Vertov, however, tried to carry his theories to their logical conclusion without realising that the path could only lead to a dead end. Believing he had something of his own to say, he gave up film reporting and began making full-length films, eschewing sub-titles and trying to give his robot camera a human character.[1] He introduced trick shots of the camera walking about on its own and of the operator preparing to take the scene which was due to arrive on the screen. In making his audiences camera-conscious, he only succeeded in rousing their resentment. In the end, of course, he had to take to staging shots which could not be snapped un-awares, but he always staged them hyper-realistically. He was obsessed with form and tireless in acquiring new techniques, but he would allow the content of his work to appear to be nothing but a record of life itself,

---

[1] Other directors in fiction films have failed in attempting the same thing: Ruben Mamoulian in the opening sequence of his version of *Dr. Jekyll and Mr. Hyde* (with Frederic March) and Robert Montgomery throughout his film *Lady in the Lake.*

captured bit by bit, as and when his cameras happened to be available at the significant time and place. In fact, he discovered for himself and dabbled in every known trick of the camera and of the manipulation of the completed shot. He knew just how to say anything on the silent screen, but he early exhausted everything he himself had to say.

In a job which at any time requires abnormal stubbornness to achieve results, Vertov was probably the most obstinate film personality of all time.[1] Since his achievements were probably more palatable in short films than in long, it is unfortunate that the silent film by which he is best known outside Russia is the full length *The Man with Movie Camera*, made in 1928 and shown privately in Great Britain early in 1931. This impression of life in Moscow from birth, through marriage and divorce to death was interspersed with personal appearances of the camera of singular precocity. Here photography and editing produced an empty display.

The film compared unfavourably with the contemporary work in the same field of the German, Walther Ruttman. His masterpiece, *Berlin*, added all the advantages to be derived from a well-fashioned script and a dramatic continuity of design and arrangement of action before the camera to the skilled use of photography and editing, which were the sole assets of Vertov's film.

Eisenstein

But Vertov's pioneer exercises in the use of camera and editing had a valuable influence in the new school of Soviet cinema. To Vertov's discoveries S. M. Eisenstein brought a rich sense of the theatre and a powerful intellect.[1] The fusion of these elements produced the three most original silent films to come out of Russia: *The Battleship Potemkin*, *October*, and *Old and New* (sometimes known as *The General Line*). In form they are comparable only to music. No one can do them justice in written description, and to reproduce illustrations from them can only serve as a reminder of a particular momentary composition. They are among the few significant silent films of all time. To keep

[1] When Vertov attended the presentation of his first sound film, *Enthusiasm*, to the Film Society of London on November 15th, 1931, he insisted on controlling the sound projection. During the rehearsal he kept it at a normal level, but at the performance flanked on either side by the sound manager of the Tivoli Theatre and an officer of the Society, he raised the volume at the climaxes to an earsplitting level. Begged to desist, he refused and finished the performance fighting for possession of the instrument of control, while the building seemed to tremble with the flood of noise coming from behind the screen.

[2] Eisenstein describes Vertov's use of slow-motion camera work in *The Man with the Movie Camera* as 'just formal spillikins and purposeless camera hooliganism'. (*Transition*, June 1930-)

faith with our subject, it is right to give a high proportion of our space to these films and their creator.

Sergei Mikhailovich Eisenstein was born in Riga in 1898 to a well-to-do bourgeois family, showed as a child a great aptitude for drawing and studied at the Petrograd Institute of Civil Engineering. He took a particular interest in the life and work of Leonardo da Vinci and from reading Freud's study of that artist began to take interest in psychology. In 1918 he volunteered for the Red Army in a fortification corps and two years later organised for his fellow-soldiers an amateur theatre company. On demobilisation in 1920 he went to Moscow and soon joined the *Proletkult* workers' theatre as designer and director under the proletarian writer, Valeri Pletnyov.

This ambitious workers' theatre movement, first of its kind in the world, derived much benefit from the influence of experimentalists of the professional theatre like Mayerkhold, whose attempts to combine stage and film have already been mentioned. In its aim to bring the workers actively into theatre practice, the *Proletkult* staged mass spectacles, celebrating *in situ* events of the revolution, as for instance *The Storming of the Winter Palace*, a pageant play which involved a cast of 1,500 actors and built up to a climax in which 100,000 citizens of Petrograd took part. Here surely are the origins of the factual climax of Eisenstein's film *October*.

Another strong theatrical influence on Eisenstein's development came from the visit to Moscow of a Japanese 'Kabuki' Theatre company, whose acting is stylised by tradition. Gestures and facial expressions are handed down from actor to actor, learnt and rehearsed like the positions in a Western ballet or the 'mudra' of the Hindu dance. The action of a 'Kabuki' play is built or mounted out of a succession of gestures and expressions just as in Japanese hieroglyphics words are built out of a combination of representative hieroglyphs: ear plus door equals to listen, or knife plus heart equals sorrow.

Following the method of Mayerkhold, Eisenstein introduced a short film into his stage production of Ostrovsky's play *The Wise Man* in 1923. Next year he wrote a film script with Pletnyov and other members of the *Proletkult* group, which he directed at the *Goskino* studio in Moscow. This film, *Strike*, won a prize at the Paris Exhibition of 1925 but was never shown in Great Britain or America, a singular misfortune for Western students of the cinema.

The necessity mentioned above, of having to use two short pieces of film, hence two different compositions, where one longer scene had been the custom before, was turned by Vertov into a virtue and by Eisenstein into the keystone of his whole theory of film construction. As he had seen 'Kabuki' mount their performances gesture by gesture, so he was now able to learn to mount his films, shot by shot, in such a way that one plus one might be said certainly to make two and at the same time to make something greater and quite different from its component parts. He studied the content of the shot, its actual length compared with its apparent length as dictated by the speed with which the human eye can assimilate a simple or complex composition in shape and movement. He analysed the conflict achieved in the juxtaposition of shots, and the variety of effect derived from the difference between a shot cut for its own value and the same cut to influence the effectiveness of those assembled before and after it.

Thus began to develop his theory of film montage. Rarely did he attempt the mere linking of shot to shot as in the more conservative schools of film construction. He believed that if he ever matched the action of one shot to the next so that the point of junction were to pass unnoticed and the flow of images to seem effortless, he was throwing away the one great asset of cinema over theatre, the force latent in the explosion of shot against shot. He created his own film-time as a form of dramatic emphasis. His most celebrated sequence on the Odessa Steps in his first masterpiece, *The Battleship Potemkin*, takes fully twice as long to show on the screen as it could possibly have taken in real life, and this at a point of climax where in the conventional film the action needs to be stripped of all but its essentials, bare and pithy and apparently taut. The secret lies in the positive creative treatment of a tragic episode of universal significance.

The Battleship Potemkin, made in 1925, was originally intended as part of a long film to mark the twentieth anniversary of the abortive revolution of 1905. Eisenstein became so absorbed in the episode of the mutiny at Odessa that he scrapped the rest of the material already shot and expanded this one sequence into an epitome of the whole revolution. The film falls into five movements:

I. *Men and Worms.* — Night. Unrest at Sea. Waves breaking. Unrest on board ship. Petty Officer strikes young sailor asleep. Morning. Meat for the mid-day stew swarming with maggots. Most of the crew refuse the call to the meal. (Steady tempo. Group shots interspersed with bold close-ups. The individual officers against the mass of the crew.)

II. *Drama on the Isle of Tendra.* — The captain orders the whole crew on deck. He threatens to shoot the mutineers. Some relent. A tarpaulin is flung over the obstinate. A firing party is lined up. Suddenly a sailor shouts an appeal. The firing party wavers, revolts. The ship's priest appeals in vain for peace. The officers run for their lives, are flung

25

overboard. One of the crew is shot. (Mounting tempo of movement and cutting, suddenly halted. Contrasting slowness follows.) The body of the dead sailor is taken in a cutter to lie in state on the end of the harbour mole.

III. *The Dead Cry Out.* — In the early dawn townsfolk begin to visit the mole. The empty steps leading down to the quays fill with people who pour along the narrow breakwater. (Masses of people with close-ups only of the dead man's head, the inscription on his breast, the money collected in his hat. Slow tempo, increasing in speed with the anger of the people. Close shots begin as individuals address the onlookers.) Fists are raised. Some officers have reached the shore and roused the troops. On board ship the red flag is hoisted.

IV. *The Steps of Odessa.* — Yawls by the dozen sail to the battleship with food, chickens, game birds, pigs, everything alive and kicking. Jubilation on board and in the bobbing boats. Jubilation among the masses standing on the quays and on the steps. Masses standing on the steps, then moving down, hurrying as a rigid line of shadows falls on the top steps. The White Guards with rifles loaded. They press on down interminably, only halting to shoot. A mother picks up her dead boy, carries him up the steps in protest and is shot down. A middle-aged woman in pince-nez tries to rally the crowd. Her pince-nez are shattered on her eyes. A woman pushing a pram is shot and falling sets the pram gently rolling, bumping down the steps until it tips over.

(Here the camera travels with the pram, the only tracking shots in the film.) Then the guns of the battleship fire on the military headquarters, toppling over the proud statues of lions that decorate the building. The people are saved. (The smooth tempo of the opening becomes faster and staccato with the conflict.)

V. *One Against All.* — The bow of the ship, crowded, becomes empty. Night. Some of the men watch, most of them rest. Morning. The fleet is reported approaching. The mutineers' committee decide to sail to meet it. Suspense. (Steady, quiet tempo, building up to rapidity with the excitement of meeting.) The fleet appears in the distance.

Potemkin loads its guns, signals: 'Comrades, join us.' No reply. *Potemkin* trains its guns, signals again, red flag flying. Then the affirmative reply from all sides. Crews line the decks and cheer as *Potemkin* steams through the fleet unassailed.

Eisenstein made magnificent propaganda here. He told most of the truth, but he omitted the rioting and arson by the civilians in the dockyards which motivated the use of troops against the populace, and he ended the film before the battleship took refuge in internment in a Rumanian port. But, choice of material accepted, Eisenstein's complete mastery of his medium in this film cannot be denied.

The continuity of the film *Potemkin* is as if the spectator is burrowing through a slice of life on the front of an inquisitive and agile drill, darting here and there in space and time, repeating a movement for emphasis, jumping in close to a face or an inanimate object, recoiling for a comprehensive view and pausing for breath after an agitated sequence. The selection of incidents and the emphasis in composition within the shot and in the juxtaposition of shots is masterly. In this film one can recognise the early manifestations of those effects, particularly of symbolism,[1] which Eisenstein developed in his later films with such intelligence and control.

Eisenstein interrupted his next production, *The General Line*, an examination of the changes to be wrought by the collectivisation of Russian agriculture, to make in three crowded months [2] of 1927 *October*, a massive film in celebration of the tenth anniversary of the revolution of October 1917. (November by the Western calendar.) Had he been allowed to give more time to it, Eisenstein would have doubtless digested his subject more thoroughly and in consequence have delivered a more shapely film with a climax worthy of the masterly first half. As it is *October* builds up, imaginatively and satirically epitomising the history of the revolution until it approaches its peak, the ten days which shook the world.[3] In dealing with these days in detail, it becomes more of a newsreel reconstruction and less of a work of art. It gets bogged down in unnecessary details for which the spectator, already half pulverised by a concentration of visual blows unparalleled in film history, has no stomach left.[4] It may be sacrilege to suggest that the Germans were right who prepared a shorter commercial version for their own market. One cannot be too grateful for this colossal experiment in film construction, great sequences of which are worthy of the highest praise, but as a whole it is fortunate that Eisenstein was to be given more time to spend on his subsequent productions, one at least of which was to achieve complete success in its own style.

In the first half of *October* Eisenstein experiments with the subjective dramatisation of ideas. His style here is utterly different from his

[1] For example, during the revolt on the battleship the use of the ship's chaplain is symbolic of decadent religion and the shots of the feet of an escaping officer treading on the keys and crushing the candlesticks of the wardroom piano.

[2] Far too short a time in Eisenstein's opinion.

[3] Title of John Reed's admirably written account of the episode and of the German version of Eisenstein's film.

[4] As the continuity of *October* is too complex to be conveyed in a short summary, a synopsis of the film is provided at Appendix A at the end of this volume.

27

straightforward presentation of events in *Potemkin*. His innovation he calls the 'intellectual cinema'. To show the fall of the czarist empire a group of workers pull down a statue of Nicholas II. Later to show the reaction against the revolution he reverses a selection of these shots, the parts of the statue reunite and the whole regains its stance on its pedestal. To satirise the ideals of the Provisional Government he analyses the slogan *For God and Country* in the manner of a political cartoonist. He represents God with pictures of the deities of current religions, following them back to the grinning token masks of the most primitive superstitions. For Country he shows crates of medals, ribbons and epaulettes. He makes Kerensky toy with a crown, overlooked by a statuette of Napoleon. When Kornilov, Commander-in-Chief of the Army, threatens to seize power, a second identical statuette appears, two Bonapartes. Kerensky flings himself childishly on a pile of imperial cushions while one of Kornilov's tanks flings itself forward into a ditch.

While *Potemkin* found favour with Soviet audiences, particularly after it had brought back renown from Berlin and elsewhere abroad, *October* turned out to be inexplicable to the simpler among Soviet audiences and infuriating to the Bolshevik leadership who adopted the term *formalism* as a derogatory description of Eisenstein's use of symbolism and his careful execution of deliberately arranged visual patterns and rhythms. Scarcely anywhere was the film allowed to be shown in its full length, and after some years it was totally forbidden both for the matter and the manner of its interpretation of history.

After finishing *October* Eisenstein returned to his study of the agricultural revolution, hampered to some extent by the fact that he was dealing with contemporary events which had not yet reached any hint of conclusion. Reviewing the work which he had already done under the title *The General Line*, he decided to scrap everything and began all over again, writing a new script which he entitled *Old and New*. Here for the first time Eisenstein dealt with fictitious characters in an attempt to humanise his subject, which at first he had proposed to present in a more abstract manner. The subject was far more difficult to tackle than those of his other films with their effectively melodramatic action. There were no fights, no gunplay, no hint of physical warfare. Instead he had to explain the advantages of the collectivisation and mechanisation of agriculture, the reactionary attitude of the poorer peasants and the antagonism of the peasant proprietors, or *kulaki* (literally fists) as the Bolsheviks called them.

For those who allow the individual artist to aim at developing and perfecting a style of his own (which freedom still belongs to a large proportion of mankind), *Old and New* is a deeply satisfying film. It has

28

humour, pathos, satire and a touching faith in the new Soviet order. It is one of the rare silent films which achieves characterisation rather than types. As is consistent with Eisenstein's work, the central figure is a peasant woman, played by Marfa Lapkina, who takes the initiative throughout in her struggle against the old prejudices and superstitions.

Marfa Lapkina lives on the screen, worn, anxious, cheerful, untidy, unwearying, completely refuting the critics who cling to the cliché about Eisenstein's concentration on mass effects and his neglect of the individual character. Like most of Eisenstein's performers she is not an actress. She has never taken part in another film. Of how many memorable screen performances can that be said?

Old and New has an absorbing subject, quieter and deeper than its predecessors.[1] And in telling his story Eisenstein has used the fruits of his previous experiences, illustrating all his theories of continuity, of montage and of pictorial composition to the full. Students will find admirable material for study in the satire and pathos of the religious procession to invoke rain, the satire of superstition and the pathos of blind faith, illustrated in a sequence which can truly be said to consist of finely composed shots which are given nearly all their point and drama in the editing. The point in the sequence of the cream separator too was achieved in the editing, though here the nature of most of the shots dictates their place in the sequence.

Old and New was a far more difficult assignment for Eisenstein than his previous films and a far finer absolute achievement. But again it was not well received by Soviet critics and audiences, who judged it too self-conscious and fanciful in its detail. However, the Soviet Government realised that his work was bringing such renown abroad for the Soviet cause and its development that they gave Eisenstein and his cameraman, Edward Tisse, permission to travel abroad to work, study and make contacts as the opportunity arose.[2]

Tisse

Eisenstein never worked with any cameraman other than Tisse until his production of *Ivan the Terrible* and has always acknowledged

---

[1] The story is told in a synopsis at Appendix B.

[2] In London Eisenstein gave a course of lectures to members of the Film Society, in Paris Alexandrov and Tisse made a short musical film, *Romance Sentimentale*, in Hollywood, with Ivor Montagu, Eisenstein planned productions for Paramount Pictures of Dreiser's *An American Tragedy* and *Sutter's Gold*, both of which were rejected as uncommercial. In Mexico Eisenstein, Alexandrov and Tisse prepared and photographed *Que Viva Mexico*, which for various reasons Eisenstein was never given the opportunity to edit. Upton Sinclair who had raised the finance, subsequently permitted the material to be issued in four films, *Thunder Over Mexico*, *Time in the Sun*, and two short films, *Death Day* and *Eisenstein in Mexico*. Eisenstein was away from the Soviet Union throughout the years 1930, 1931, 1932. He returned to find the sound film firmly entrenched.

29

the contribution which this brilliant photographer has made to his films. In his youth Tisse had studied painting and in 1914 was making short travel films. He became an official war photographer and in May 1918 went over to the service of the Soviet Central Cinema Committee. He continued to work as a reporter for the newsreels and thus developed that sense of film editorial continuity which is essential for all film cameramen who want to be remembered for their films rather than for the composition of individual shots within the films.

Eisenstein's three masterpieces are interesting to study for the development of their camera work. *Potemkin,* largely consisting of exterior scenes shot in daylight, is striking for its linear composition, while the later films abound in more and more complex and subtle examples of the composition of light and shade. In *October* Tisse never hesitated to use light artificially to create dramatic effects without attempting to account for a realistic origin for the source of light. *October* contains the remarkable sequence of the crowd awaiting Lenin's arrival at the Finland Station and listening to his first public speech. The restlessness and agitation implicit in this almost motionless crowd is largely conveyed by the deliberate moving of beams of light (as from searchlights) back and forth over the mass of anxious faces. It is only the night and the open air that is actual. Tisse strung up his lights all over the square for the attack on the Winter Palace, and he did so in a manner that would make a military tactician shudder. Thus works the artist who has graduated from the school of actuality. The camera artist brought up in the theatrical tradition of the film studio would probably have chosen to shoot these night scenes in daylight, using filters in front of his lenses. But he would have produced a much less harsh negative and a gentler effect, and this would have clashed with the mood of bitter conflict which was the chief characteristic of the subject itself.

In the quieter style of *Old and New,* Tisse again used light unrealistically to emphasise a change of mood. In the sequence of the cream separator not only do choice of facial expression and editing express the change from distrust and prejudice to pleased acceptance. Gloomy lighting also gives place to brightness and sparkle as the machine begins to fulfil expectations. At the climax the brightness of the lighting is totally at variance with the natural possibilities of light values in the old-fashioned shed where the machine is installed.

Tisse's work in silent films reached its highest quality in the Mexican material which emerged as *Thunder Over Mexico.* This film was assembled by conventional Hollywood editors who tried to fathom Eisenstein's scenario and notes. Tisse's contribution to the material alone makes it memorable.

30

Eisenstein is an intellectual of bourgeois stock, a socialist by conviction rather than by birth. There is nothing in him of the worker or peasant, and the criticism with which much of his work has been received has been unable to change his natural characteristics. Therefore his historical reconstructions have always been more acceptable to the Bolsheviks than his presentations of current life, for whereas a worker or peasant has the advantage over Eisenstein of being able to interpret the contemporary Soviet life of the masses from within, no man from any stratum of society can do other than interpret history from the outside.

Dovzhenko

By contrast with Eisenstein's intellectual approach to the agricultural revolution, it is interesting to compare with *Old and New* the Ukrainian film *Earth*, made by the Ukrainian peasant and painter, Alexander Dovzhenko. Born in 1894, Dovzhenko first earned his living as a school teacher and later as a cartoonist on a newspaper. In 1925 he began writing film scenarios and then from 1927 to 1929 he directed his first three films: The *Diplomatic Bag, Zvenigora* and *Arsenal*. His fourth, *Earth* (1929-30), brought him international fame and was his best and last silent film.

Earth rose out of the heart and bones of its maker. Dovzhenko did not need to approach the subject or study the background. Rather the film flowed out of his consciousness.[1]

It has a slow gentle tempo which is disturbed and speeded up only at moments of conflict or of enthusiasm. The story is simple. Among the fertile undulating landscapes, an old man dies 'as old men must', while the apples ripen on the trees and the corn thickens in the fields. The kulaks defend their boundary fences against the encroachments of the collective farm. The co-operative has bought a tractor which arrives after the customary breakdown with which Soviet peasant films were wont to make fun of the industrialists.

In Dovzhenko's original, the tractor's radiator boiled over and was replenished with the urine of its enthusiastic purchasers, but this episode was removed by the Soviet censors. The old man's grandson, Vassily, starts reaping the corn with the help of the tractor, the women bind the sheaves, a threshing machine goes to work and soon the villagers are making bread. Vassily then goes ploughing and drives across the boundaries of a kulak's farm. Work ceases for the day, lovers sit watching the sunset, animals graze, the land rests. Vassily walks home in the moon-

---

[1] When Eisenstein's second peasant film *Bezhin Lewis* failed (in 1937), Dovzhenko referred to Eisenstein as a 'city man who does not know the country. Formalism [he went on] often crops up when the author lacks knowledge of the life which he is portraying.'

light. Happily he begins to dance, a minute figure in the distance kicking up the dust of the lane. Faster and nearer he dances—ecstatic, then suddenly falls. Horses start up from their grazing. A man runs away in the distance. Vassily lies still, the dust floating in the air above his body. He has been shot.

In the cottage, his father watches beside the body. The village priest arrives, but the father rejects the idea of Christian burial. The villagers come and take the body, making a procession through the fertile fields, ignoring the church where the priest prays alone. The body lies on an open bier and the branches of the trees laden with fruit brush the face as it is carried by. The young kulak, the murderer, runs to the cemetery, shouting that it is he who has killed Vassily. He dances among the graves in a parody of Vassily's dance, but the people ignore him too. Rain falls, glistening on the crops and the fruit. The clouds pass and there is peace again and sunshine on the raindrops.

The film is a chain of fine pictures, too slow for many tastes, but lyrical without a touch of sentimentality. After an interval of fifteen years, the visual and emotional impact of Vassily's dance in the dusty moonlight still excites the memory. Dovzhenko the peasant never achieved in his military and industrial subjects the satisfying sureness of *Earth*.

Training Courses

It was mentioned earlier that among the first acts of the Government Cinema Committee was the establishment in 1918 of training institutes in Petrograd and Moscow. It soon became the excellent custom to co-opt to the staff of these institutes practising craftsmen of the top rank as and when their work in active production allowed. Writers, directors, cameramen and art directors came to regard it as an honour to be invited to give lectures and also to present the problems of current production to students attached as apprentices to the various film studios. Eisenstein became a lecturer at the Moscow Institute and undoubtedly has had as much influence on the new generation through his writings and teaching as through his much criticised productions. From 1934 to 1937 he evolved a four-year course for students of film direction which proved almost too exhaustive to observers like Dovzhenko.

The latter maintained that a year of training in theory and a year of practical apprenticeship are sufficient to set the beginner on the road to film direction. Eisenstein, however, would not let a student graduate until he had produced and directed a film on paper, with evidence of research into the background of the subject, costume designs, designs and plans of settings, a detailed shooting script, sketches of every composition and diagrams of every movement of actors and camera in every setting and location. In addition all students received instruction in general knowledge, including history, philosophy, political economy and mathematics.

The director of the Moscow Institute since May 1944 is Lev Vladimirovich Kuleshov. From the earliest days of the Revolution, Kuleshov has represented the most generally acceptable progressive element in Soviet film production. He was born in 1899 and got his early training in the Khanzhonkov Studios as assistant to a film director called Bauer, whose name is among the few respected by the survivors of the Revolution. Bauer was no czarist, and his independence of outlook and personal integrity barred him from much commercial success.

In those days, the creative editing of films was known as the American style in acknowledgement of the pioneer work of D. W. Griffith. In 1918, working for the Cinema Committee, Kuleshov made further experiments in film editing, taking advantage of the enforced intervals between productions, when no film stock was available, to discuss and experiment in the new grammar and syntax of the film strip. In 1920 he began lecturing on his theories at the Moscow Institute.

Pudovkin

One of his students was Vsevolod Pudovkin, an older man by six years, a chemist from Moscow University whose career had been interrupted in 1914 by voluntary military service and by several years spent as a prisoner of war in Germany. Pudovkin wanted to be an actor, but with the traditional thoroughness of the Russians Kuleshov put his students through the mill of understanding all the other jobs in films as well. Pudovkin quickly assimilated Kuleshov's theories, learning how it was possible by skilful editing to make non-actors appear to give convincing performances and how even to bend an actor's performance to purposes of which the actor had no knowledge at the moment of performance. His strong visual sense and his scientific training conspired to divert him from a career as an actor, now proved of lesser importance,[1] towards the more creative work of film direction.

After graduating, Pudovkin joined the Mezhrabpom-Russ Studios, playing in Kuleshov's comedy, *The Extraordinary Adventures of Mr. West in the Land of the Bolsheviks*, a satire on the conventional American horror of Communism. His own production work began in 1925 with a factual film, *The Mechanism of the Brain*, a straightforward demonstration of the research work on conditioned reflexes at Professor

---

[1] With reference only to the silent, not the sound, film.

Pavlov's Laboratories in Leningrad. In 1926 he made a two-reel comedy, *The Chess-Player*, into which he edited shots of the expert Capablanca, so arranged as to make him appear to play a part in the development of the story. During the next three years, Pudovkin made three full-length dramatic films which were to provoke the greatest emotional reaction among international audiences of any Soviet films up to the present day.

While Eisenstein's films provoked discussion and respect (or the reverse), their direct appeal was to the intelligence first and only through the intelligence to the emotions. They were connoisseur's pieces in the main. But Pudovkin's films appealed directly to the emotions of the mass audience and only secondly to their intellect. They were passionately clear and simple. To Pudovkin the most important element is the story. His attitude to his subject is personal and emotional, not detached or intellectual. In these silent films he used mixed casts of actors and non-actors, the latter to bring verisimilitude in those parts where realism was more necessary than the ability to act. Pudovkin's editing technique, derived from Kuleshov, he describes in the essays on *Film Technique*[1] which he wrote as lectures for the Moscow Institute in 1926.

While Eisenstein preached the principle of montage as *shock*, the collision of two factors giving rise to a *concept*,[2] the Kuleshov school described their milder principle as *linkage*, the linking of a chain of shots into a *narrative*. Eisenstein's method was appropriate for films concerned with the direct representation of ideas, Pudovkin's for those concerned with the effects of ideas and events on human relationships. In practice, the appeal of Pudovkin's conflicts of personalities proved more universal and immediate than Eisenstein's abstractions.

Mother, Pudovkin's first dramatic film, and *Potemkin* were both concerned with the Revolution of 1905. *The End of St. Petersburg*, his second, and *October* were both designed to commemorate the tenth anniversary of the 1917 Revolution, some sequences literally covering the same ground. In London, *Mother* stirred its private audiences to unusual enthusiasm, while its successor roused the spectators to a demonstration which provoked questions in the House of Commons.

The former was taken from the novel by Maxim Gorky and is remarkable for the performance of the actress V. Baronovskaia as the mother and of the actor Nicolai Batalov as the worker son who goes to prison because of his mother's political inexperience. In the stark, brutal climax, the son is shot while trying to escape and his mother is trampled to death by cavalry as they ride down the workers' demonstration.

---

[1] Translated by Ivor Montagu; Gollancz, London, 1929.
[2] See *The Film Sense* by S. M. Eisenstein, translated by Jay Leyda; Faber and Faber, London, 1943.

Baronovskaia gave another fine performance in *The End of St. Petersburg*, the story of which, by Nathan Zarkhy, is a thread of fiction woven into an accurate representation of the history of the period. The result is a larger, looser film than *Mother* and in its different style much more successful than *October*. In *Petersburg*, it is the conversion to socialism of an ignorant peasant lad, played by I. Chuvelev, which illustrates the history of the period. In this film, Pudovkin was the first to achieve the blending of a fictional foreground over a factual background with complete success. In order to achieve this sense of reality, Pudovkin selected his cast with an eye to their social background. His business men and stockbrokers, for instance, had been business men and stockbrokers under the old regime. In spite of this critics outside the Soviet Union complained that these figures in the film resembled caricatures in looks as well as behaviour. It is sometimes difficult to decide where to recreate facts in a film and where to meet the doubts of ignorant spectators by pandering to their illusions.

Pudovkin's next silent film was *The Heir to Jenghiz Khan*, better known under its German title *Storm over Asia*, adapted from a story by Novokshenov. Set in the steppes of Central Asia, this story of the White forces operating against the Partisans, irregular troops, of the Revolution, was diffused in the film by the use of too much factual material of life in a market town and of a great religious festival in a Buddhist monastery. The material was less relevant to the theme than the historical background of *Petersburg*, and in giving it too much space, Pudovkin achieved a film with a powerful beginning and end but a languorous middle section. In England, the reception of the film was further complicated when the uniforms worn by the White troops were recognised to be British. Fears that the private performance would provoke further questions in Parliament proved to be groundless, however, though none of Pudovkin's silent films were licensed for general public showing throughout the country.

The main story of the film concerns a young Mongol trapper (played with great sincerity by V. Inkishinov, later to become a film star in France) who takes a valuable silver fox fur to market, is cheated by a European trader and causes a riot. White troops are called in, but Bair the Mongol escapes and joins the Partisans in the hills. While a religious ceremony is being held in the town, fighting breaks out in the hills over the seizure of some cattle by the Whites. Bair is captured and shot. His belongings are searched and the translation of a paper in an amulet identifies him as a direct descendant of Jenghiz Khan. The White general has Bair's body brought in, and finding Bair still alive they patch him up and present him to the rebellious locals as their new king. Bair remains passive till at the ceremony he recognises his fox fur adorning the neck of the general's daughter. He snatches it back, turmoil breaks out, a Mongol is shot, Bair goes berserk, smashes up the ceremonial hall and gallops away on horseback to the Partisans. He rallies them and during a great symbolic tempest leads them against the White imperialists, whom they drive from the land.

Other progressives

Among directors whose work in writing, photography and editing shows the influence of the progressive school are the team of G. Kozintsev and Leonid Trauberg, and the latter's younger brother Ilya. Kozintsev and Trauberg combined these methods with the results of their experiences influenced by their highly theatrical experience gained on the stage in their 'Factory of Eccentric Actors'. This group had brought the techniques of circus and music hall to the presentation of straight drama. Their best known film was *New Babylon,* a story set in and around a Paris department store, in which Pudovkin appeared as a shop assistant. The film was made in Leningrad in 1929 to mark an anniversary of the Paris Commune of 1870. While using all the emphasis of camera and editing of the progressives, they also stylised their acting and settings, producing a result which greatly enriched the scope of the Soviet cinema.

During the same year Leonid Trauberg's brother Ilya, then aged twenty-three, directed an effective adventure film, *The Blue Express,* from a story by L. Yerikhonov. All the action took place in and around the express train, meant to be symbolic of China, the locale of the story, moving rapidly towards capitalism or communism. The editing largely contributed to the visual impression of the train's progress. Although settings and costumes were realistic, the writing and acting were consciously exaggerated and melodramatised. The result was an allegory, which the less sophisticated enjoyed merely as an exciting thriller.

Other directors like Boris Barnet (known particularly for his comedy *The Girl with the Hat Box* which starred Anna Sten) emerged from the influence of the progressive school unscathed and settled down to turning out films in the conventional tradition of 'getting on with the story and joining the bits as they come'. Silent films of that kind tend towards telling too much of their story in sub-titles and illustrating only the geography and movement of the tale, just as the conventional sound film tends to illustrate its 'commentary' or dialogue rather than to visualise its subject and use the sound track for comment and effects. The contribution of the progressive group to the development of the international silent film cannot be overestimated. It ranks with that of **D. W. Griffith** and **Charles Chaplin** in America and with the 'golden age' of the German silent film.

The coming of sound

It is unfortunate that this group did not go forward to hold its own in the development of the sound film. The intention existed since 1928, but its execution was interrupted partly by Eisenstein's travels abroad and partly by the setback which Pudovkin suffered over his production originally titled *Life is Beautiful,* and later renamed *The Story of a Simple Case.*

While he was preparing this story of the amorous adventures of a member of the Red Army, Pudovkin was told that he could make it the first Soviet full-length sound film. He therefore re-drafted it in terms of the theories which he had discussed with Eisenstein and others, photographing as much as possible silent in anticipation of creating the appropriate sound tracks later according to the demand of his new script. Then he found that the sound engineers were not ready for him.[1] Thereupon he arranged his material for the third time, silent once more. The result dissatisfied him and he contrived to have it withdrawn from circulation after three days of showing at Leningrad and one day at Moscow. With characteristic generosity, however, he organised for the Film Society one performance in London. From dim memory there survives an impression of an ineffective story and of small details of masterly visual and editorial virtuosity: for example, the tiny detail of the putting on of an overcoat from which the audience received the impression of overwhelming, enveloping warmth. And there was a moving impression of a delirium, built out of a cascade of factual images of natural objects and processes, first of drought, decay, death and then of the living power of water welling up, breaking the dead earth crust forcing new growth.

By 1933, the year in which Pudovkin showed his first sound film *Deserter* and Eisenstein returned from abroad, the film craftsmen in Russia as elsewhere had anchored the microphone to the film camera and were in full pursuit of the presentation of characterisation which had been largely denied them by the nature of the silent film.

[1] The inventors, Tager and Shorin, had been working on systems of variable density and variable area recording respectively since 1926, and Tager was able to record a commentary for a newsreel as early as August 1929 and to make musical and effects recordings for silent films, like Shostakovich's score for *Alone* in 1930. But the first synchronous recording of speech and picture was not achieved until the end of that year in Nikolai Ekk's full-length film *The Road to Life.*

This enlargement of technical scope supported the revolt against the former line of development, now condemned as *formalism*. The new policy, known as *socialist realism*, aimed at a simple naturalism, and adventures in individual virtuosity were considered unnecessary if the subject explained itself in plain statement.

THE
SOVIET SOUND FILM

by

Catherine de la Roche

Towards socialist realism

THE TRANSITION from silence to sound in the Soviet cinema took place during the first Five Year Plan, 1928-32, when the USSR threw its entire energy into socialist construction after the upheavals of the first decade of the Revolution. All the arts were then emerging from a turbulent period of experiment and reorientation and entering the era of socialist realism. As the new way of life was becoming stabilised, so, too, was a new style in art.

In the cinema the origins of socialist realism are to be found in the masterpieces of the silent cinema: in Eisenstein's historical epic without a fictional plot; in Pudovkin's drama based on the relationship between individuals and society; in Dovzhenko's epical drama with people as symbols of great social ideas. They established the dominant realistic trends which ran parallel until they were eventually synthesised in the broader concepts of socialist realism.

At the end of the silent period various minor trends, either formalistic or naturalistic, had also come into being. Practically all the film makers tried one or other of them in their search for a form to fit the new content of their pictures. At that time the chief aim of all the arts was to define the new 'positive hero', no longer a subversive revolutionary, but a self-confident, optimistic member of socialist society, and the opposite of the futile, superfluous 'negative hero' of nineteenth-century Russian art. In the cinema this could only be achieved by creating living characterisations in place of the 'types' and symbolical figures of the silent film. It became clear that non-realistic tendencies could only lead the cinema away from its goal. The didactic method of the agitational propaganda film; naturalism, with its stress on external imitation of reality instead of an interpretation of it; formalism, which neglects or obscures content—all these were a hindrance to film makers searching for a way to interpret the story of their times by bringing real

39

characters to life and thus developing the film medium as art. The conflict which developed between these trends and the stronger trends of realism was the last stage in the dialectical growth of the cinema towards socialist realism.

This conflict was nearing its climax when sound revolutionised the cinema. Those who had the vision to see its possibilities soon realised that they were precisely of the kind needed for the development of the style that was being sought; the spoken word would help in the creation of a cinema of living characters. Others, it is true, feared that the talkie would encourage naturalism or theatricality. The significant thing is that, in the USSR, the technique of sound film had to be mastered in the light of newly reassessed artistic aims. The story of the Soviet sound film is, in fact, the story of the evolution of socialist realism in the cinema.

The principles of socialist realism reached maturity and definition in about 1932. In April of that year all literary and artistic organisations in the USSR were reformed and coordinated, and soon after this the term 'socialist realism' became common currency. Briefly, this is art which has its sources in the life of society and is created for society as a whole. Its aim is to interpret reality, past or present, in the light of socialist ideology. It excludes egotism in any of its manifestations, but encourages individuality of artistic expression. Every dramatic form — satire, fantasy, comedy — is applicable, provided it is used as a means of expression and not as an end in itself. Socialist realism is not a rigid dogma. Its many elements evolve and change together with the society in which it exists.

First steps in 1931

Research into the theory of sound was begun by the engineer P. Tager of the Moscow State University in 1926. At that time the country was short of materials and technicians, and it was not until 1929 that the recording equipment he designed, the Tagephone SGK-5, was installed in the main studios. By 1930, when the Five Year Plan was well advanced and the industrial strength of the nation had grown, new sound studios, picture theatres, etc., were being built all over the USSR, and the expansion of the film industry was accelerated.

The first sound feature film, *Alone*, written and directed by Gregori Kozintzev and Leonid Trauberg of the Leningrad studios, appeared in 1931. It was made as a silent film and had music and effects added subsequently. Telling the story of a Leningrad girl who went to the snow-covered Altai mountains as a village schoolteacher, it proved to be the most controversial film of the year. In it the directors departed from the

40

stylisation of their silent pictures, without, however, attaining the realism which had become their aim. They succeeded in bringing human beings to the fore, and, by analysing the particular—an individual girl's work and conflicts, they gave an idea of the general—the heroism of everyday life. But, in giving a stylised impression of Leningrad as a city of magical charm and contrasting it with the bleakness of the Altais, they exaggerated the sacrifice motif, and overlooked the typical optimism which sent young pioneers to the far corners of the USSR.

Golden Mountains, an exposure of the avarice and prejudices which had taken root in peasant psychology as a result of centuries of exploitation, also concentrated on the human element. It was made in Leningrad by Sergei Yutkevich, co-founder with Kozintzev and Trauberg in the 1920's of *Fex*—Factory of Eccentric Actors—and was his first important work as director.

Meanwhile, in Moscow, Nikolai Ekk, graduate of the Film Institute, made the famous *Road to Life,* about a band of child delinquents who were transformed into an orderly, self-governing little community when put to work building a railway. *Road to Life* was notable for its acting, which compensated for weaknesses in the script and made it a picture of tremendous human appeal. N. Batalov of the Moscow Art Theatre was remembered for years as the gay, intelligent tutor, and so was the Asiatic boy, I. Kyrla, as Mustafa, leader of the gang who had to overcome many conflicts before he was reformed. *Road to Life* was also an early example of the possibilities of sound effects, especially in the night scene on the railway where Mustafa was murdered: the metallic noise of wheels and Mustafa's carefree song, as he rides alone in a rail hand-cart; further along the line, the stillness of the night, broken only by croaking frogs and the light clinking of tools while the murderer loosens a rail; then Mustafa's distant song becoming louder and louder as he approaches danger.

Socialist construction themes

The next few films were a direct result of the April 1932 reorganisation mentioned earlier. They attempted to show the new human relationships which were the motive power of socialist construction. *Counter Plan,* written and directed by Friedrich Ermer and Yutkevich in Leningrad, was the most significant among them because of its influence on future Soviet pictures. Ermler was a Communist Party worker before he began filming. During the silent period he was criticised for Freudianism, impressionism and other 'isms', and disconcerted many by his unorthodox longing to use words, to show characters saying one thing while thinking another, to reveal the mobility of thought, the pathos and passion of

41

political speeches. For Ermler the advent of sound was the fulfilment of a dream.

The plot of *Counter Plan* was stereotyped and somewhat didactic. Three stock characters—the political leader, the saboteur and the unenlightened old worker who gradually assumes his new responsibilities as owner, together with the nation, of the factory where he works—are involved in building a turbine in record time. The novelty of Ermler's treatment was in the humour with which he endowed the characters, especially the political commissar, usually represented as a solemn model of virtue, and in the way he counterpointed dramatic situations with comedy. A theme which had hitherto been treated with intense earnestness was here deliberately broadened and humanised. But the scenario was weak and the humour superficial, instead of arising from real characterisation. Ermler's first talkie was therefore more interesting thematically than cinematically.

As in *Alone* and *Golden Mountains*, the music for *Counter Plan* was written by Dmitri Shostakovich. He gave each of the sound effects in the workshop passages specific emotional values by building his musical phrases around them. Symphonic passages with a psychological quality accompanied the dramatic scenes. Shostakovich made his early contributions to the cinema at a time when he, too, having abandoned the grotesque and technological in music, was advancing in a new direction.

In Kiev, Alexander Dovzkenko, poet of the Ukrainian cinema, made his first talkie, *Ivan*. It was the story of the pathos and romance of building the Dnieper dam and of its effect on a typical peasant who became transformed into a politically conscious citizen. Despite its familiar theme, this was not a stereotyped production—Dovzhenko's pictures never are. But it failed in its chief object, which was to unfold the story through the changes in Ivan's psychology. Dovzhenko dwelt too long on the grandiose rapids which were being conquered, on the dynamic rhythms of cranes and excavators and engines, on the fantastic patterns of steel girders, illumined by arc lamps during the night shifts, losing sight, now and again, of his characters. Nevertheless, Dovzhenko's burning convictions inspired every inch of the film, and its underlying idea came vividly to life. *Ivan* was full of Ukrainian lyricism and temperament.

Barnet, Kuleshov, Pudovkin

The Moscow pioneers of the silent film, Lev Kuleshov and his former pupils, Vsevolod Pudovkin and Boris Barnet, came out with their first talkies in 1933. Barnet's *Borderland* was the most successful. He was a comedy director, known for his affinities with Charles Chaplin, especially in his faith in the importance of actors and of those miniature roles which come to life in a single flash on the screen. Set in a frontier town during the first World War, *Borderland* was a story of many characters and of their various national prejudices which were swept away by the Revolution. 'It would be pointless and dull', wrote the critic I. F. Popov, 'to try to define the genre of *Borderland* in old terms. Ours is a bold and youthful age. We can destroy existing forms of art because we have acquired new criteria. Old subdivisions cannot prevent us from achieving new integrations. In *Borderland* the elements of comedy are mixed with those of drama and even tragedy.' These mixed elements were inherent in the clearly defined central theme developed by Barnet, and for this reason he succeeded in combining them into an organic whole. This was a direct advance towards socialist realism.

Kuleshov, on the other hand, concerned himself little with socialist realism in *The Great Comforter*, based on O. Henry's story. Made in the tradition of his silent films, tense, disciplined, logical, *The Great Comforter* was notable for the virtuosity of its 'natural actors' and of its montage. Kuleshov concentrated on a single aspect of the story, the collision between reality and illusions, reducing it to pure abstraction. The film had intellectual power but little emotional appeal, and though acknowledged by crities as brilliant of its kind, it was the kind which was disappearing from the Soviet cinema.

The possibilities of sound fired Pudovkin's imagination as soon as it was invented, and in 1928, together with Eisenstein and Alexandrov, he published a paper the main thesis of which was the development of sound as a counterpoint to the visual image and not as a duplication of it. In *Deserter*, about a dockers' strike in Hamburg, Pudovkin demonstrated how montage could be combined with sound, thereby re-establishing movement as an essential of the cinema. He showed how film dialogue could be made to differ from theatrical dialogue by concentrating the camera on the listeners, bringing in the speakers only if their behaviour added something to their words. The classic example of sound counterpointing image was the scene of the dockers' fight for their red flag. A joyous, triumphant march was heard throughout the changing fortunes of the struggle, symbolising the faith which would make the dockers victorious. Pudovkin was acutely aware of the possibilities of sound for achieving socialist realism, a concept which his own work had helped to develop. But in this respect *Deserter* was less successful, chiefly because it was a story of events, not characters.

Expansion and new standards

In 1934 the Soviet sound film entered its best period which was to last until the war. The major trends, instead of leading in different directions were now synthesised within the broad outlines of socialist realism, and, as a result, the variety in styles and subject-matter increased. Film makers of all kinds of talent knew where they were going. All films were designed for mass audiences, whose cultural level had risen and whose numbers had increased. The 'kinefication' of the USSR during the first Five Year Plan had trebled the number of projectors, bringing it to 27,000.

New talent was attracted into films, especially stage actors. Now that the cinema was concentrating on characterisation, actors assumed first place in film production. In fact, the art of directing talkies evolved out of the collaboration between directors and actors, and here the artistes of the Moscow Art Theatre played a significant part. They create their roles by *experiencing* rather than outwardly portraying them, experiencing them so completely as to be able to suggest a character's past biography, the contradictions in his psychology and the faintest undercurrents of emotion. Their sober, realistic method was peculiarly suited to the film medium. Pudovkin, whose theories on film acting were based on it, believed it could be developed even more fully in the cinema, with its close-ups, than in the theatre. Be that as it may, some of the Moscow Art Theatre's principles took root in the cinema, influencing the actors working in the permanent units of various film directors as well as those who came from other theatres.

Literary classics

Some of the year's major productions were based on classics. These are chosen from the point of view of their social value in present-day life. In filming them, the chief aims are, firstly, to re-interpret a classic in the light of contemporary knowledge, and, secondly, to create a genuine cinematic equivalent, as distinct from either literal translation or exploitation of a plot for introducing extraneous ideas.

Storm, made by Vladimir Petrov, one of the newer Leningrad directors, was the best. Petrov did not fundamentally revise A. N. Ostrovsky's play on which it was based. But he did revise the traditional stage interpretation of Catherine, the tragic heroine, as 'a ray of light in the kingdom of darkness', revealing her not only as a victim of her environment, but also as a product of it: rebellious yet submissive, passionate yet fatalistic. And he put greater emphasis on the greed and bigotry of the 'dark kingdom' of the Volga merchant folk. In this way the characters were put more clearly into relation with their social background. *Storm* was essentially a film of personalities, magnificently portrayed

44

by Moscow Art Theatre actors, with Alla Tarasova as Catherine (the most coveted role in the Russian theatre).

Judas Golovlev, made by Alexander Ivanovsky, also in Leningrad, was a condensed but somewhat weakened version of Schedrin's novel about a miser whose indifference to his fellow-beings became so complete as to amount to a negation of all existence except his own. Vladimir Gardin, veteran actor and founder in 1919 of the First State Film Institute, gave a notable performance in the title role, but the screenplay failed to bring out the social indictment inherent in Schedrin's work.

In *Petersburg Night,* made in Moscow by Grigori Roshal, the treatment of the classical material was different. The hero was one of those 'composite' or 'generalised' characters of whom there were to be many in Soviet films, and the screenplay was a social reinterpretation of a theme which Dostoyevsky had developed only from the psychological viewpoint in two of his stories. It was the theme of wasted talent, of the failure of the artist striving for superficial success and seeking recognition from the fashionable society which spurns him. The hero was made a prototype not only of Dostoyevsky's two characters, but also of the composer Mussorgsky and others whose talent eventually perished in the social conditions of Petersburg life. As in one of Dostoyevsky's stories, he was a violinist. The music by D. Kabalevsky was, therefore, a primary factor in the construction of the screenplay, and also one of the film's best qualities.

Amo Bek-Nazarov, leading Armenian director, who filmed *Pepo* (1935), a play by the greatest Armenian dramatist, Gabriel Sundukian, approached his task on the same general lines. More particularly, he was concerned with developing an art which would be, in Stalin's words, 'national in form and socialist in content'. In the Armenian cinema this still meant a struggle against the old tendency towards the superficially exotic and picturesque as distinct from a genuine interpretation of national aspirations and culture, which was the aim. *Pepo* was notable not only as a vital reinterpretation of Sundukian's classic about the conflict between the Erevan underworld and the rich merchants of pre-revolutionary times, but also as a film which was deeply national in spirit and characteristic of its epoch. Beautifully rendered Armenian music contributed to the film's expressiveness and style.

Musical Comedy

Meanwhile Gregori Alexandrov, who had worked with Eisenstein on his silent films and subsequent American ventures, made *Jazz Comedy* in Moscow. Together with *Storm* and *Petersburg Night,* this film won first place for Soviet films at the 1934 international film exhibition

45

in Venice. *Jazz Comedy* was in effect a combination of the American gag with a Soviet background and syncopated Russian folk melodies. The plot was simple in the extreme, the comedy arising solely out of gags, not characterisation. Nevertheless, the film was full of vitality and laughs. On the whole the experiment met with approval, though many critics doubted whether so radical a departure from traditional Russian comedy, which is based on characters, was the right course to take. Alexandrov wanted to create a gay but satirical genre, with anti-social types as targets for the wit and an optimistic element in the socialist hero, but he did not succeed until later in the decade. His next film, *Circus*, made in 1936, was a sentimental though sincere musical on the subject of racial tolerance, which contributed little to his and his permanent unit's work in developing socialist comedy. Among the leading personalities of his unit are Lyubov Orlova, singer, dancer and the most popular comedy film star in the USSR, and I. Dunaevsky, a composer famous for his choral songs. Many of the stirring melodies he has written for films reached such popularity as to become national songs of Russia, notably the *Fatherland Song* from *Circus*.

Historical revolutionary epics

At the end of 1934 the brothers Sergei and George Vassiliev, young directors of the Leningrad studios, completed *Chapaev*. It was the first triumph of socialist realism in films, representing a new synthesis of the total experience of the Soviet cinema, just as Dovzhenko's work had been, to a certain extent, a synthesis of the epic and dramatic styles created by Eisenstein and Pudovkin. The story of Chapaev's division which fought on the Ural front during the Civil War, develops the wider theme of the formation of the Red Army out of separate, undisciplined partisan units. Only those elements of the story which emerge as typical when viewed in historical perspective have been used. In writing the screenplay the Vassilievs endeavoured to achieve simplicity, eliminating everything 'decorative' or even 'illustrative'. In this respect, as also in its photography and setting, the film is ascetic. The drama is developed entirely from within and is intensely concentrated. The characters are shown as the motive force behind the events, which in their turn motivate the actions of the characters.

Chapaev, who was born of the people and raised by them to leadership, is first shown in his relationship with the masses. He is seen in battle and then during a pause (making it clear in his inimitable dialogue what he thinks of partisans who lose their rifles) as a commander of colossal natural authority, fearless, talented, artful, humorous. Then

46

his character is developed through his conflict, which becomes a friendship, with the political commissar and through the more bitter conflict within himself to overcome a partisan's anarchic habits and become a politically conscious Red Army commander. Here Chapaev's vanity, ambition and ignorance collide with his honesty and wisdom and with the willpower of the commissar. A corresponding process is traced in other characters, while others again, notably the commissar and the counter-revolutionary officer, are revealed as formed but complex personalities. A score of character sketches gives identity to the masses. The drama of all these people is integrated in the epic events which never become a mere background. In the famous psychological attack against Chapaev's division, for instance, not a single foot of film is 'wasted on illustrative' panoramas; the sequence is so constructed as to make the characters clearly involved in each phase of the action, whether it is seen in close-up or in long shot.

Chapaev recaptured the spirit of its epoch completely. Boris Babochkin, actor of the Academic Theatre of Drama, who had no physical resemblance to Chapaev and deliberately ignored many of his well-known mannerisms in order to crystallise his essential characteristics, gave a performance true enough to convince the whole country, including Chapaev's relatives and Red Army veterans like Marshal Voroshilov. When early in 1935 the Soviet cinema celebrated its 15th anniversary, Stalin sent a greeting to the film workers, wishing them new successes similar to *Chapaev*.

We from Kronstadt (1936), made in Moscow by Efim Dzigan, was the next greatest success. Like Chapaev it was an 'optimistic tragedy' about men who died not hopelessly, but believing in a noble and triumphant cause. They were the marines of the Baltic Fleet who fought a dual battle during the Civil War—the armed battle and the struggle to conquer the evil within themselves, the stale remnants of a way of thinking and feeling which had no place in the dawn of a new age. Unlike *Chapaev* the film had no leading characters. As in Eisenstein's epics the mass was the hero, but because this picture was made in the era of socialist realism, each sailor was given a vivid individuality. Here again the background and events were perceived not as separate phenomena, but as a materialisation of 'the fire and the storms raging in each man's breast and as an expression of the ideas which possessed their minds.' (I. F. Popov.) Though the film had few words and little music (composed by N. Krukov), it was notable for the excellence of both. The script was written by V. Vishnevsky, a brilliant playwright who was an enthusiast of the film medium and collaborated tirelessly with Dzigan in exploiting its possibilities. Hence the unity of the production and the remarkable unbroken élan which carries it forward from start to finish.

Formation of a Bolshevik

The transformation of a carefree young proletarian into an irreconcilable Bolshevik was the theme of the first big talkie from the Tbilisi studios, *Last Masquerade* (1934), made by Michael Chiaureli, one of Georgia's leading directors. In his youth Chiaureli had been a sculptor and a painter and, perhaps for this reason, his films are known for a monumentality in the delineation of sequences and for their design. *Last Masquerade* covers a period from before the first World War to the sovietisation of Georgia. As in most of Chiaureli's films the episodic story has moments of profound solemnity, vivid bursts of passion and some political satire. The film's success led to Chiaureli being introduced to Stalin.

The same theme was developed by Kozintzev and Trauberg in the *Maxim* trilogy, their greatest contribution to cinema. It consists of *Youth of Maxim* (1934), *Return of Maxim* (1937) and *Vyborg Side* (1938). The first shows how the gay, naïve Petersburg labourer Maxim becomes a revolutionary in 1910, the second deals with him as a seasoned political worker in 1914, and the third shows how, knowing nothing about accountancy but much about dealing with people, he became Finance Minister during the civil war. The directors began working with their cast before the script was finished. Boris Chirkov, originally a stage actor, invested the title role with so much charm and fire that the fictional Maxim became something of a national hero. The unit was a strong one all round, and the efforts of all were concentrated on developing the characters. The ace cameraman, Andrew Moskvin, who works on all Kozintzev and Trauberg's films, having already renounced his famous expressionist and symbolical effects when photographing *Alone*, now achieved realism of great vitality, especially in his unobtrusive dramatisation of the squalid, unpicturesque workers' suburb of Petersburg. Always a master of portraiture, he found more scope than ever in the Maxim films, which were noted for his close-ups. Dmitri Shostakovich further developed the use of sound effects as an integral part of his music, which was exceedingly dramatic.

Contemporary themes

From 1935 on some of the outstanding films of each year dealt with an increasing variety of contemporary subjects. Friedrich Ermler made *Peasants* (1935) which, unlike the 'intellectual' silent films about village life, was appreciated by the peasant masses. As has happened on many occasions in the history of the Soviet cinema, the film was inspired by a speech of Stalin's. Ermler tried to depict the current problems of

48

collectivisation as Stalin had interpreted them in 1933. *Peasants* was an advance, as compared to *Counter Plan* in the psychological genre Ermler was to achieve in his best pre-war films, *Great Citizen.* Part 1 (1937) and Part 2 (1939).

The character of Shakhov, hero of these films, was modelled on that of the Bolshevik leader Kirov. The films trace his activities in rationalising heavy industry from the NEP period to 1934, when he was assassinated. Through Shakhov, Ermler tried to reveal the essential characteristics of a Bolshevik leader, not only as regards ideology, but especially as regards morality, and at the same time to show the psychological difference between him and the counter-revolutionary agents who opposed him. Because the screenplay by M. Bleiman and M. Bolshintzov was primarily a drama of characters and of the conflicts between them, Ermler was not afraid of making full use of philosophical and political dialogue. And because much of the theme was developed through dialogue, he devised a technique which, at that time, was uncommon in Soviet films. He wanted uninterrupted continuity in each scene so as to give the actors freedom of movement, and he wanted both camera work and cutting to remain unnoticeable. *Great Citizen* was therefore shot in long strips with a maximum use of camera movement for rhythm and close-ups, and with little quick cutting. The camera angles were from the audiences' viewpoint (no sudden reverse shots). Occasionally, when Ermler required a 'commentary' from the camera, he allowed it to emerge from its unobtrusiveness, as in the last scenes when Shakhov walks through a doorway beyond which the assassin awaits him, the camera races to a close-up of the closing door handle, just as it clicks with finality. By these means Ermler made of *Great Citizen* a production of great dramatic tension and fine performances, especially by the actor N. Bogolyubov in the title role.

In *Airmen* (1935), Yuli Raisman, of the Moscow studios, brought out the romance and the lyricism of routine life at an aerodrome. An early enthusiast of sound, he had made one of the 1931 experimental talkies, *The Earth Thirsts*, about the irrigation of the Turkmen desert, which is said to have influenced King Vidor's *Our Daily Bread.*

Airmen was remarkable for the skill with which Raisman integrated the background of aerodrome life—sound of aero engines, shadows of aircraft overhead, the constant bustle of people at their jobs—with the story of contrasting attitudes to flying among the chief characters. Raisman's film of M. Sholokhov's famous novel about a collective farm, *Virgin Soil Upturned*, was one of the best productions of 1939.

Seven Brave People (Leningrad, 1936) brought Sergei Gerasimov to the fore as a young director primarily concerned with the theme of contemporary youth. He had started as an actor in Kozintzev and Trauberg's unit, playing villains ('because of my appearance, not my nature', as he once put it) in several films, including *Alone*. He trained a group of young film actors who subsequently became permanent members of his unit. Some of them, including Tamara Makarova, Oleg Zhakov and Peter Aleinikov, soon became famous. Together with this unit Gerasimov explored the possibilities of 'close-ups in words', devising his scripts in such a way as to unfold the plot through action and to reserve the dialogue solely for characterisation. Referring to *Seven Brave People*, Pudovkin wrote: 'I think Gerasimov is first in discovering the right form for screen dialogue.' Gerasimov and his unit evolved one of the most individual styles in the Soviet cinema. Accent is on understatement and simplicity. The drama and the passion are revealed by suggestion, seldom directly. This was typical of the tone among 'komsomols' (communist youth) of the 1930's, with whom Gerasimov shared a loathing of pretentiousness and big words.

Seven Brave People was a story about geologists wintering in the Arctic. Gerasimov's next picture *Komsomolsk* (1938) dealt with the building, entirely by youthful workers, of the new town of the same name on the river Amur in Siberia. And *New Teacher* (1939) was the drama of a young teacher, struggling to win the confidence of the villagers among whom he had elected to work, and of his love for one of his pupils. However diverse the stories of these films, they all had the romance of pioneering, the same fine team work by the cast and vividly laconic dialogue. They also had outstanding individual performances, especially by Tamara Makarova, feminine lead of all three. She is particularly admired in the USSR for the charm of her voice and intonations and for her quiet sincerity. And Boris Chirkov, who was decorated for his work in the *Maxim* films, gave another fine performance in the title role of *New Teacher*.

Stories of the Revolutionary Period

New stories connected with the Revolution continued to be filmed each year. Lev Arnstam, previously a musical director in Leningrad, chose this background for the two successful films he directed before the war. He is one of the few directors who is not afraid of showing the emotions of his characters openly and directly, risking the kind of situations which approach, but do not cross the borderline of sentimentality. His theme is friendship. *Girl Friends* (1935) was the story of the touching youthful friendship between three front-line nurses, and of their lyrical romances. This film made the actress Zoya Fedorova famous. *Friends* (1938) dealt with the friendship between men of

50

different races in the days when the flood of revolutionary events engulfed the mountain folk of the Northern Caucasus breaking down the barriers of old prejudices.

1937, twentieth anniversary of the Revolution and close of the second Five Year Plan, brought a spate of outstanding pictures, several of them connected with the Revolution. Among these was *Baltic Deputy*, a development in the direction of drama of the historical style created in *Chapaev*, just as *We from Kronstadt* had been a development of it towards the epic. If the character of Chapaev, while typifying many of the partisan leaders was essentially biographical, 'Polezhaev' in *Baltic Deputy*, though primarily a personification of the botanist Timiriazev, was much more of a 'composite' character, hence the fictitious name. Timiriazev, 'poet of science', was not the only Russian professor who supported progress before it became clear which side would win in the Revolution. For him, as for Mendeleyev, Pavlov and others, his vocation, science itself, was on the side of progress, though most of his colleagues did not share his convictions. So 'Polezhaev' was a character typifying a minority, and the opposite of the professor who became stereotyped in earlier Soviet fiction as an old man 'who wonders during three acts whether to acknowledge the new system or not, acknowledging it just before the last curtain'.

The story shows how 'Polezhaev', spurned by his colleagues and lonely, finds friends in the sailors of the Baltic Fleet who elect him as their deputy to the Petrograd Soviet. *Baltic Deputy* was essentially a collective achievement. It was made in Leningrad by the First Komsomol Film Brigade, headed by the young directors Alexander Zarchi and Joseph Heifitz, who had declared that the theme of youth was their primary interest. However, their early pictures devoted to it were all 'promising failures'. But it is not as paradoxical as it appears that their first triumph should have been the story of a 75-year-old professor, for his most endearing characteristics were his turbulent youthfulness and his enthusiasm for a young cause. And it may well be that the restless, humorous 'Polezhaev' came so convincingly to life precisely because he was brought into being by a young team which (on their own admission) was entirely captivated by his charm and affinities with themselves.

The film had a good start in a fine script by L. Rachmanov and the directors who understood how to provide the central character with movement, both spiritual and physical. The cameraman, M. Kaplan, scrupulously avoided effects. He had a tough job. Three-quarters of the scenes took place at night, 'Polezhaev' was played by 32-year-old Nikolai Cherkassov in heavy make-up and incessantly on the move. Concen-

51

trating on his eyes and attitudes, Kaplan found he could capture Cherkassov's vital performance best by photographing him in medium shot, taking only two close-ups in the entire film. *Baltic Deputy* was also a personal triumph for Cherkassov. He had started as a mime in the Marinsky Theatre, Petrograd, and at first he preferred eccentric dancing and comedy, believing that 'any dilettante could walk and talk in drama'. He was soon to distinguish himself in dramatic plays, nevertheless, and when he came to the cinema, it was with a genuine interest in it as a new and independent medium.

Another successful film set in the October Revolution was Raisman's *Last Night*, about two families who had been acquainted and find themselves on opposite sides in the conflict.

Actors impersonating Lenin and Stalin

Before 1937 there had been no talkies with actors portraying Lenin and Stalin. But on the strength of the experience gained in filming other national heroes, the attempt was made, and *Lenin in October* (1937) was the first of several films which can justly be claimed as achievements unique to the Soviet cinema. Characters, one of recent memory and the other living, were recreated in such a way as to convince hundreds of personal friends and millions of citizens in a country where all media of communication (including newsreels) had for years been familiarising the public with the personalities of the two leaders, their faces and their voices.

Lenin in October and its sequel *Lenin in 1918* (1939) were made in Moscow by Michael Romm, a young director whose rise to success was exceptionally swift. After his silent film of Maupassant's *Boule de Suif* (1934), he made the talkie *Thirteen* (earlier 1937), about Red Army men in the Karakum Desert, both of which were mature, polished productions. Romm is known as a man of wide culture whose work has clarity and assurance.

Recreating Lenin's character meant showing him as the guiding genius of the Revolution. The success of the films, especially the first in which Lenin was still in hiding, was due largely to the skill with which A. Kapler, the scenarist, and Romm worked out the interrelation between Lenin and the masses, and to the logic of the transitions from intimate scenes to the epic ones which, according to the cameraman, B. Volchek, were on a scale never before attempted in the Soviet cinema. The actor, the late Boris Schukin, was thus provided with first-class situations, and he rose to the occasion. Schukin was an actor of the Vahtangov theatre and a typical representative of the realistic 'Russian school of acting'. One of the characteristics of this school is the art of combining the comic with the tragic, and this probably helped Schukin in finding the right balance between the humour and authority, the irreconcilability and the humanity of the character he was portraying. His film experience included important roles in *Airmen* and in Vera Stroeva's *Generation of Conquerors* (1936). It had long been Schukin's ambition to play the part of Lenin, and for some years he had studied the mass of available material about him. He had acquired an uncanny sense for the cadence of Lenin's speech, and was able to improve certain lines of the already admirably written dialogue.

In Leningrad, Sergei Yutkevich filmed N. Pogodin's play 'Man with a Gun' (1938) which had several episodes with Lenin, the actor M. Strauch playing the role. Yutkevich then made the biographical film *Jacob Sverdlov* (Moscow, 1940) with Strauch again in the role of Lenin. He did well, but his roles were smaller than Schukin's.

Meanwhile, among the two or three actors who were attempting to impersonate Stalin, Michael Gelovani, who, like Stalin, is a Georgian, was the most successful. A distinguished actor of the Georgian stage and screen, Gelovani is known for his humour, fire and simplicity. His first appearance as Stalin was in *Great Dawn* (1938), made by Chiaureli in Tbilisi. He played the same role in several other films, including Lev Kuleshov's *Siberians* (1940), M. Kalatozov's *Valeri Chkalov* (1941), about the famous airman, and in the brothers Vassiliev's *Defence of Tsaritsin* (1942), but though he was decorated for his achievements, he felt he had only given an external portrayal and continued working in preparation for a deeper characterisation.

Further expansion

During the second Five Year Plan the 'kinefication' of the USSR increased the network only by a thousand projectors, bringing the total to about 28,000. At the end of 1938, 54 per cent of these were sound projectors. By 1941 the third Five Year Plan (interrupted by the war) had brought the figure to 31,000 of which 11,000 were in towns and 20,000 in villages. The number of attendances for 1939 was estimated at 900 millions. The rate of production had increased bringing the average number of feature films made yearly from 1936-40 to between 40 and 50. New equipment factories were now supplying most of the needs of Soviet studios in apparatus and raw stock (though the quality of the latter was not yet up to standard), considerably reducing the need for imports. Printing laboratories in Moscow, Leningrad, Kiev and Tbilisi ensured the simultaneous production of some 1,200 copies of each film upon its release, and progress was made in the art of dubbing films into and from the languages of the national republics. Even more important was the vastly increased number of qualified specialists regularly emerging from the film institutes and technical schools and the many young units which had gained experience inside the studios. By 1939 100,000 people were engaged in the Soviet film industry. The Stakhanovite movement (socialist competition) played a considerable part in improving efficiency in all departments.

As the cinema expanded, so, too, did the scope of themes, many of which could not be dramatised within the limits of a single screenplay. Series films, therefore, became a feature of the Soviet cinema in the latter 1930's. Three of these have already been mentioned. Another, the Gorki trilogy, was the most outstanding early contribution of 'Soyuzdetfilm', the new children's film studio.

Children's cinema

In 1936 the famous Mezhzabpom studio in Moscow, where directors Pudovkin and Kuleshov, cameramen Golovnya and Ermolov, designers Kozlovsky and Egorov and many other leading film artistes had grown up, was converted into 'Soyuzdetfilm'. Some of the existing personnel stayed on. New blood was drawn in to reinforce it. The new units thus formed set about evolving 'a great cinema for small people'. At first the studio concentrated on stories *about* children, instead of tackling a wider range of themes *for* children. The most charming of these was Vladimir Legoshin's *Lone White Sail* (1937), taken from Valentin Kataev's adventure story about children during the Civil War.

In 1938 came *Childhood of Gorki* which was followed by *Out in the World* (1939) and *My Universities* (1940), all based on Maxim Gorki's autobiographical stories. These films brought Mark Donskoi to the front rank of the Soviet cinema, as a young director of great sensitivity, good taste and an exceptional flair for handling children. His choice of subject was not accidental. Gorki's themes—the dignity of man, the inspiration of discovering pride and talent in the oppressed, indignation at seeing talent wasted under oppression—these themes had always inspired Donskoi. In the Gorki films he developed his own individuality.

The Gorki trilogy had some magnificent performances by old and young alike. In the first two films, Varvara Massalitinova, one of Russia's greatest stage and screen actresses, made a half-pagan, earthy, pure, gay-and-sad grandmother straight from Gorki's pages. In the first film, little I. Smirnov as the crippled boy filled his role with pathos which had not the slightest trace of self-pity in it. Donskoi understands children well enough to realise that they give of their best when they are allowed to share in the knowledge of what is at stake in a job. The moment they understood the point of the script, they found it comparatively easy to laugh and cry and express their emotions spontaneously. Donskoi's next picture was *Romantics* (1941), about the first school organised by Soviet pioneers for Chukchee children in the Far Eastern Arctic. This film, too, had enchanting and highly intelligent performances by the children, all of them Chukchees.

Children's films are produced under the supervision of educational experts, and the special children's theatres in which they are exhibited are run by specially trained personnel. A characteristic of most of the 'Soyuzdetfilm' productions is that they are equally interesting for grown-ups and are made on the same scale and with the same (and sometimes greater) efficiency as features in other studios. The subjects soon began to cover a wide range: fairy stories and folklore (*Humpback Horse*, 1941, director A. Rou), historical (*Salavat Yulaev*, the Bashkir national hero, 1941, by Y. Protazanov, who had filmed Ostrovsky's *Without Dowry* here in 1936), biographical (*Lermontov*, about the nineteenth-century Russian poet, 1943, director A. Gendelstein) and modern stories such as Gaidar's *Timur and his Comrades*, 1940, director A. Razumny.

Historical themes

In the later 1930's, as a result of Stalin's initiative, a number of films were devoted to the history of Russia and other member nations of the USSR. The episodes chosen were those which, according to Soviet historians, represented the most heroic, patriotic and progressive moments of the nation's past, irrespective of the subsequent interpretation of them by historians of the ages. If Alexander Nevsky was canonised as a saint by the Orthodox Church, and if Ivan the Terrible had come to be remembered only as a tyrant because nineteenth-century historians had sensationalised his bloody deeds at the end of his reign, the films concerned themselves with both men as *people's* leaders and with their part in the people's struggle for unity, freedom and against aggression. Alexander was not shown as a saint in *Alexander Nevsky*, nor Ivan as a maniac, either in the first part of *Ivan the Terrible* which was released, or in the second, the scenario of which was published, but the film of which was banned. The broad principles of the reinterpretation of history are similar to those governing the reinterpretation of the classics and the interpretation of revolutionary and contemporary themes: a summing-up of the most typical elements of the epoch; selection of incident from the viewpoint of its importance in the light of contemporary knowledge; dramatisation of the whole by creating credible and, again, *typical* characters.

First of the magnificent historical canvases were Vladimir Petrov's *Peter I*, Part 1 (1937), and Part 2 (1938), based on the late Alexei

Tolstoi's historical novel. Exhaustive research for the production had started in 1934. The films dealt with Peter's struggle against feudalism, his wars to secure Russia's outlets to the Baltic and Black seas, his efforts to introduce Western European civilisation into Russia. The theme was the conflict between the old and the new. And this conflict was crystallised in superbly living characters: Peter, robust, dynamic, hard-working, gay, ruthless, impersonated with tremendous temperament by N. Simonov; his half-idiot son, Alexis, cruel and cowardly, played with his usual virtuosity by Nikolai Cherkassov; Menshikov, loyal, but a rogue, portrayed with great style by Michael Zharov, and a long list of others.

In Moscow Sergei Eisenstein who, since his return from abroad, had been contributing to the Soviet cinema as professor, theoretician and critic, scored a new triumph as director with *Alexander Nevsky* (1938). It was a direct development of the epic style he created in his master-pieces of the silent cinema. Like these it was a film of a mighty national movement, of great masses of people inspired and united by an idea. Its thirteenth-century story centred round Prince Alexander who, as chosen leader of the people of Novgorod, vanquished the Teutonic knights on the ice of Lake Peipus, was told as a legend. The characters, boldly drawn and unencumbered with psychological detail, were monumental figures. The cadence of their dialogue (very sparingly used), designer I. Spinel's superbly simple architectural sets, Sergei Prokofiev's deeply national music—all were conceived as they are imagined today and as they survived in folklore. There was too little historical data to go on, and, in the case of the music, the fragments which have survived no longer had the meaning they probably had 700 years ago. The production created its own 'period' style, broad and simple and heroic. Certain available details were changed. Eisenstein did not stress the tragic aspect of the famous battle on the ice which, according to the chronicles, was 'red and black with blood'. Following the colossal tension of the initial onslaught, the scene of the hand-to-hand fighting developed into a feat of supreme optimism. Sunlight, glittering snow and the grinning faces of the Russians all built up the effect of victorious self-assurance. This, too, came from legends of gay, indomitable Russian warriors. Optimism was made the leitmotiv of the production.

Alexander Nevsky was a patriotic epic, pulsating with life and full of humanity. Eisenstein with his old-time colleague, cameraman Eduard Tisse, again revealed their genius for pictorial composition and gran-diose panoramas, but their treatment was more realistic. If many of Tisse's characteristic methods—swiftly alternating angles, contrasts in light and shade, etc.—could be detected, they were more unobtrusive

56

and subordinated entirely to the action. The more dynamic the scenes, the more vivid and active the camera work. In the calmer scenes, on the other hand, the lighting, the composition and the angles were toned down, and overall, the spectator's attention was not deflected by the virtuosity of the photography.

Vsevolod Pudovkin, who had made *Victory* in 1938 from the late Natan Zarchi's last script about the record Soviet round-the-world flight, also turned to historical themes. From a script by the famous author Shklovsky he made *Minin and Pozharsky* (1939) about the butcher Minin and Prince Pozharsky who became popular leaders in the fight against the Polish invaders during 'the Time of Troubles' of the seventeenth-century. As might have been expected of Pudovkin, this was essentially a film of characters and their part in a popular movement. Pudovkin's next film was *Suvorov* (1941) about the last victories of Russia's greatest general who, in his old age, routed Napoleon's forces in the Alps, crossing the St. Gothard Pass. Suvorov, who had worked his way up from the ranks and whose sayings and witticisms fill pages of Russian history, was something of an eccentric. The film was built around his character, but it had two heroes: Suvorov and his Army. The actor N. P. Cherkassov (not to be confused with his namesake in the title roles of *Baltic Deputy* and *Alexander Nevsky*) gave a dazzling performance as Suvorov in a film of big-scale events with dialogue in magnificent style. This was the first big success in sound film of Pudovkin, his co-director M. Doller and cameraman A. Golovnya—the team which had worked together in the silent film period.

From the Kiev studios came *Bogdan Hmelnitzki* (1941), an epic about the seventeenth-century Cossack Hetman who saved Ukraine from Polish domination and united Ukraine with Russia. It was directed by Igor Savchenko, who had made one of the earliest musical comedies *Harmonium* in 1934. The scenario was by the famous author Alexander Korneichuk, the photography by Yuri Ekelchik, Dovzhenko's colleague, and the enormous cast included N. Mordvinov and M. Zharov—an exceedingly strong unit. Ekelchik, ignoring the opportunities for decorative effects which exist in costume films, concentrated, as ever, on the characters, making some outstanding portraits, and on relating his broad, poetical views of the land of Ukraine with the people who were born of its freedom and fought in its defence.

Civil War themes

Bogdan Hmelnitzki was, to a certain extent, influenced by *Chors* (Kiev 1939), the film which resulted from Stalin's advice to Alexander Dovzhenko in 1935 to make 'a Ukrainian *Chapaev*'. That year he had

57

completed *Aerograd*, a film about construction in the Soviet Far East. In *Chors* he returned to the theme which has become inseparable from his name—Ukraine and the immortality of her people. The poetical force of Dovzhenko's films (he writes his own screenplays in the tradition of Gogol's and the poet Shevchenko's epics) is probably unsurpassed in the Soviet cinema. Even the reviews of his work by many leading writers, including the playwright Vishnevsky in 'Pravda' and the author Shklovsky in 'Kino', read like prose poems inspired by a kindred passion. Dovzhenko had participated in the events depicted in *Chors*. In 1918-19 he fought with the Ukrainian partisans who, like Chapaev's division, became founder members of the Red Army. The tears, the laughter and the glorious songs of the Ukrainian people, 'heroic, intelligent, mocking, lyrical, who move through the entire film, through fire and smoke and snows and boundless cornfields', are Dovzhenko's own. He made *Chors* a film about the future as well as the past, about the aspirations for which the heroes gave their lives. At moments the figure of Chors (played by E. Samoilov) assumed the quality of legendary heroes of long, long ago, a timeless quality, and at the same time he and his devoted comrade Bozhenko (I. Skuratov) and many others were real, full-blooded characters of their epoch. *Chors* was full of pathos and romance, it had the sunny Ukrainian humour and richness which is characteristic of Dovzhenko's work.

If in *Alexander Nevsky* Eisenstein had increased the depth of the screen, Dovzhenko with Ekelchik broadened it in *Chors*. It had sweeping panoramas with action in the foreground, farther away and in the background taking place in patterns of varying rhythms in order to convey the immensity of the events and of the human will which set them in motion. The symbolism and the didactic notes of their earlier films had vanished. Except in a few scenes satirising the enemy (which were adversely criticised), *Chors* achieved simplicity.

The proportion of big and successful pictures had grown at the end of the decade. Among those devoted to the Civil War was *Volochaevsk Days* (1937), set in the Soviet Far East and made by the Vassiliev brothers. Another, *Zangezur* (1938), by Amo Bek Nazarov, came from the Erevan studios in Armenia.

Musicals

Comedy, the production of which had been encouraged in various ways, including comedy script competitions, had improved considerably since the beginning of the 1930's, but it has always been regarded as one of the most difficult and least successful genres in Soviet films. In *Volga-Volga* (1938) Alexandrov and his unit had a typical modern theme—the activities of an amateur musical society. They created some simple, but quite natural characters, and made good use of the Volga countryside. The film was full of gaiety and had some very funny slapstick. It also had some more of Dunaevsky's delightful music. This film was a successful example of the kind of socialist comedy Alexandrov had been aiming at, with a typical optimistic background and the laughs often at the expense of somebody or something unpraiseworthy. It was followed by *Bright Path*, a Cinderella story, made in 1940.

Ivan Pyriev, who had made a good dramatic film in *Membership Card* (Moscow 1936), developed a different type of musical comedy, built on ordinary workaday stories. The first two, *Rich Bride* (1938) and *Tractor Drivers* (1939), dealt with life in Ukrainian collective farms. Both had good, witty scripts by E. Pomeschikov, leading Ukrainian scenarist who had graduated from the screenwriting faculty of the Film Institute. They were joint productions of the Kiev and Moscow studios. Many in the cast, especially the soprano Marina Ladynina, star of Pyriev's unit, were not Ukrainian, nor did they pass for such. However, the films had tempo, gaiety and charming tunes (by Dunaevsky and the brothers Pokrass). In 1941 Pyriev made *They Met in Moscow* with a script and lyrics by the poet Victor Gussev. The dialogue was rhythmic, some of it in blank verse, and the language and style of the production inspired by Russian folklore. Much of the film's charm lay in the verse which was unpretentious and well delivered. *They Met in Moscow* was centred round a livestock exhibition in Moscow and traced the simple love story of a Georgian shepherd and a Russian girl working on a pig-breeding farm, who met at the exhibition.

In Leningrad A. Ivanovsky made *Musical Story* (1940), about an amateur singer who makes good, with Zoya Fedorova as the girl who loves him. Love of music and an understanding of it was felt throughout the story which had a profusion of good musical numbers, mostly Russian classics. The Kiev studios made two experimental operatic films which did not, however, rank with the best of their product.

New contemporary themes

A number of topical films about the foreign scenes were making their appearance in the second half of the 1930's. A. Minkin and G. Rappoport of Leningrad produced *Professor Mamlock* (1938), about racial persecution in Nazi Germany. In Moscow, A. Macharet made *Soldiers of the Marshes* (1938), about German concentration camps. This film was noticed for the good work of the young cameraman E. Andrikanis. In order to bring out the difference in expression on the faces of the Nazis and those of their victims unobtrusively, without caricaturing the Nazis, he used a hard, close-range lens for the Nazis and ordinary ones for the victims. Also, as often as possible, he photographed the heroes on the background of the masses, while the Nazis were shown alone and isolated from the humanity they were exterminating.

G. Roshal made *The Oppenheims* (1939) on a similar theme. In 1937 he had made *Dawn in Paris*, an historical picture of topical interest. Its hero was the Polish revolutionary Dombrovsky, hero of the Paris Commune, whose name was inscribed on the banners of the Foreign Legion, who had fought for Madrid. Efim Dzigan, at the head of a brigade of three young directors, made *If War Comes Tomorrow* (1939), a rousing call to the nation to be prepared.

Among the most successful films on the contemporary Soviet scene of this period was *Member of the Government* (1940), made by Zarkhi and Heifitz. It traces the career of a woman (played by Vera Maretskaya) from a collective farm, who becomes a member of the Supreme Soviet. *Great Life* (Kiev, 1939) was devoted to the miners of the Donetz Basin and brought the young Ukrainian director Leonid Lukov into prominence. Reviewing this film, A. Stakhanov, famous originator of socialist competition, acknowledged it as a true and deeply moving account of the Stakhanovite movement and rationalisation of labour. The film had strong characters, fiery, enthusiastic Ukrainians, and through them it showed the conflicts and the changed attitude to labour which resulted in the new human relationships among miners. From the Ashkhabad studios came *Dursun* (1940), directed by E. Ivanov-Barkov, which traced the story of the Stakhanovite movement in the cotton plantations of the Turkmen SSR. This was one of the few big successes to come from the studios of the Central Asian republics where the cinema was developing steadily but slowly.

Some of the best films at the turn of the decade were based on classics. In 1938 the young Byelorussian director, I. Annensky, made Chekhov's 'The Bear'. Though Byelorussian directors such as V. Korsch and A. Fainzimmer had produced several fine films, few of these were on Byelorussian national themes, and as a result, the national cinema of Byelorussia was comparatively undeveloped. In 1941 Sergei Gerasimov filmed Lermontov's poem *Masquerade*, the only departure from contemporary themes in Gerasimov's career. It was a production in grand style, with Lermontov's verse superbly rendered and recorded. In the same year G. Roshal completed a film of Gorki's *Artamonov and Sons* a story showing the futility of a pre-revolutionary merchant family whose only interest was profitable business. The film depicted their gradual mental decline as the years passed and they changed from youthful slenderness to a middle-age spread and finally to the thinness of old age, their discontent and frustration growing with their riches.

Popularity of the Cinema

The first decade of the Soviet sound film brought the cinema of ideas to the masses. If some of the early silent film masterpieces had been abstract, the best talkies, from *Chapaev* onwards, were essentially human, dramatic, vital. Through their heroes they found their way to the hearts and imaginations of the broad public in town and country alike. The ideological movie had become box office. It has never been the intention of Soviet film makers to 'talk down' to the masses or to lower the standard of the cinema to suit the least educated sections of the public. For one thing the level of education itself was rising constantly and rapidly during the Five Year Plans. For another, the role of the cinema is a leading, not a following one: it is used as a medium of enlightenment, it is designed to set ever higher standards both artistically and ideologically. If only the best pictures fully achieved their aims, while some of the average ones were naïve, or clumsy or just dull, the reason for this was an insufficiency of talented or qualified film-makers, not policy. The policy was to develop the film medium as a living, popular art which would be true enough to inspire the whole nation. The *Maxim* trilogy, *Baltic Deputy, Chors* are among the many examples of this kind of cinema and also of the success of socialist realism in films. Pictures such as these were popular and they satisfied exacting critics.

All the time the links between the cinema and national life were being strengthened. Production news has always been given in the Press at length. Film festivals and anniversaries, stills exhibitions and displays of designers' sketches and models, lectures and script-writing competitions —all these grew in popularity. The weekly correspondence received by leading directors, actors, etc., is enormous and often constructive. Eisenstein, Romm, the Vassilievs and many others have recorded numerous instances of valuable historical data and intelligent suggestions being offered by people from all corners of the USSR. Many film workers engage in social activities: actor Nikolai Cherkassov and director Michael Chiaureli, for instance, were elected members of the Supreme Soviet in the 1930's.

The volume of film criticism increased correspondingly. Its level has been high ever since the silent film period. It is characteristic of Soviet criticism that in addition to the regular critics, leading directors and other film people analyse each other's work in the national Press as well as in film periodicals. The broad public has constantly had opportunities to read Pudovkin on Ermler, Eisenstein on Romm, Roshal on Dovzhenko, and so forth. The numerous debates and conferences among film people, often controversial, are reported at length. Criticism is severe; film-makers publish self-criticism on their own films. Not one of the pictures referred to in the sound section of this book (which are only the major productions) has escaped adverse criticism of some kind. Criticism in the national Press as well as in 'Cinema Art', 'Soviet Art' and other cultural periodicals, is *cinematic* criticism, as distinct from dramatic or literary appraisals of a film's story or the actors' performances. In addition a number of serious books and monographs on the best productions have appeared regularly. The public is thus accustomed to read appraisals of the contributions of cameraman and composer as well as of director and actor. There is lively contact (as Eisenstein has written) between the masses and the film workers who, in their turn, draw their inspiration from the masses.

At the same time contacts between the cinema and other arts and between the national cinemas were being widened. If in the early days of sound the cinema borrowed more from the theatre than it gave in return, after *Chapaev* and other successes the cinema began exercising a certain influence on the theatre. The national cinemas, while primarily concerned with developing their own national art, have never confined themselves to this work. There has always been interchange of personnel between studios—Dovzhenko and others have worked in Moscow, Russian artistes have worked in most national studios, occasionally two studios have engaged in joint productions.

Some general points

The growth of the industry was accompanied by periodical reorganisations, one of the most important being that of 1938 when a central film committee was formed. As a result of its initiative, work in all departments was stimulated and rationalised. An exchange of ideas and experience between the art departments of all studios, for instance, resulted in certain basic structures of sets being standardised, a measure which increased the designers' scope besides achieving economy. Many of the ideas adopted had been originated by Sergei Kozlovsky (*The Deserter, Lermontov*), chief art director of the children's film studio who had introduced prefabricated sets into Soviet studios.

Scenic design has always been a strong department of Soviet film production. The famous theatrical designer Vladimir Egorov (*We from Kronstadt, Virgin Soil Upturned*) brought the realism of the Moscow Art Theatre to the cinema when it was in its infancy, and developed the best traditions of Russian painting and graphic arts in films. The Kiev designers Maurice Umansky (*Chors*) and Y. Rivosh (*Bogdan Hmel-nitzky*), collaborating with cameraman Ekelchik, evolved a simple realistic style in recreating the vivid Ukrainian scene, discovering its typical features and freeing them from old-fashioned extravagances. Talented designers in every Soviet studio have played a leading role in developing the cinema as art.

However, their role, as that of the cameramen, gradually became more unobtrusive. If in the 1920's composition, outline, lighting effects, etc., could exist as independent elements in a montage scheme, in the 1930's, when characterisation became paramount, the function of all the cinema's component arts became subordinated to it. Cameramen abandoned their striking angles and their concern with the photographic possibilities of some fascinating background, and concentrated on the actor. It was this preoccupation—more than the technical inventions which, by increasing the camera's mobility, decreased the need for incessant cutting and changed the techniques of photography and editing—this preoccupation caused the seeming disappearance of the 'virtuosity' of Soviet camerawork. In fact the photography of the greatest masters, old and new, was on a high level. Moskvin (*Maxim* trilogy), Tisse (Eisenstein's films and *Aerograd*, etc.), Kaplan (*Baltic Deputy*), Golovnya (Pudovkin's films), Gardanov (*Peter I*), Ekelchik (*Chors*) and others, often solved bigger problems in talkies than ever existed in the silent film. The measure of their success was the fact that their photography was unnoticeable in itself except to experts.

The interrelation between all the arts in the cinema was gradually modified. A cinema of characters depended on the development of screen drama. Screen writing became recognised as the foundation of good cinema. But despite the achievements of directors who are writers in their own right (Eisenstein, Dovzhenko, the Vassilievs, Gerasimov, Kozintsev and Trauberg, etc.), professional scenarists (E. Gabrilovich: *Last Night*) and authors (A. Tolstoy: *Peter I, Golden Key*, etc.; V. Shklovsky *Miin and Pojarsky*) and others, the scenario department was always short of creative writers. The 1938 co-ordination resulted in a strengthening and extension of the scenario departments in all the studios with a view to developing screen-writing as an independent creative art, but it has always been (and still is) difficult to persuade the biggest writers and new talent to devote themselves to screen-writing. In 1940 a separate script studio was set up in Moscow where experienced writers and beginners started work under the guidance of an editorial board consisting of leading authors such as K. Simonov and B. Gorbatov, scenarists, critics and film producers.

63

Documentary

Throughout the pre-war period, documentary and newsreel studios belonged to a joint organisation. They had common roots and, in their transition to socialist realism, which meant a transfer of stress from things and events to people, they remained closely akin. In becoming humanised, documentary did not become fictionalised. While making use of some of the experience of the feature film, documentary did not move much closer towards it. And the feature which, in the USSR, also had its roots in realism, partly documentary, did not move any closer towards documentary.

Dziga Vertov's three *Songs of Lenin* (1934), one of the best films of its kind, is an early example of socialist realism in documentary. Compiled from historical newsreels with additional coverage, the film shows the optimism and the pathos of socialist construction as Lenin's work. Three Central Asian songs about him were illustrated in the three parts of the film, which has something of the poet Mayakovsky's lyrical ardour. It was built up on associations: the associations of Lenin with the events and of the people with their achievements. Instead of the impressionism of Vertov's famous 'Kino-Eyes', this film had deeper feeling and emotional appeal. Another full-length documentary based on historical newsreels was *Land of Soviets* (1938), by Esvir Shub, one of the biggest documentary directors who has specialised in historical documentaries. In her next film *Spain* she collaborated closely with the playwright Vishnevsky and the composer Popov, believing that documentary can gain from using some of the methods of the feature film, without sacrificing the authenticity essential to documentary.

Probably the most characteristic documentaries of the 1930's were those devoted to big topical events. Cameraman Arkadi Shafram who was with the 'Chelyuskin' Arctic expedition in 1934 obtained a remarkable record of it in appalling conditions. He worked to a script, under the guidance of Mark Troyanovsky, veteran cameraman of the Arctic, who had filmed the Soviet flight to the North Pole. Vladimir Eshurin photographed the Abyssinian war. Ace cameraman Roman Karmen with B. Makaseev spent over a year in Spain during the Civil War. Karmen was the only cameraman to record the last days of resistance in Madrid, when the city was in flames. In the USSR he is known not only for his fine newsreels and portraits, but also as a journalist and for his easy, characteristic verbal newsreel interviews. In Ukraine, cameraman Konstantin Bogdan has made some brilliant records of the typical day-to-day life on collective farms.

From the material of these and hundreds of other cameramen, together with special coverages, have been compiled the full-length documentaries which record most of the important events during the Five Year Plans. They include Bliach's *Shanghai Document* and *Kirov*; Dziga Vertov's *Symphonie of the Donbas* and *Lulluby*; Kaufman's *Aviation March*; E. Alexandrov's *Stalin Constitution.* Others were devoted to physical culture parades, the Fleet, the Ferghana Canal, construction of the great industrial plants and so on. In addition the numerous newsreel issues and documentary shorts were also compiled from this material, including separate sports and cultural issues. The Cultural newsreel, which has excerpts of ballet, concert and theatrical performances in all the national republics, has evolved a good technique, all its own, for indoor newsreel coverage. There is a special children's newsreel, 'Pioneer', which shows children at work and play in all the republics, so that those in the Arctic regions can have an idea of the life of those in sub-tropical Central Asia and so forth.

Scientific and technical

The demand for technical and scientific films grew enormously during the Five Year Plans. In 1932 new studios for their production were opened in Moscow, Leningrad and Novosibirsk, with facilities for animated diagrammatical work, quick and slow-motion filming, photomicrography, etc. Films began to be more carefully angled for special audiences: schoolchildren, the broad public, or specialists. By the 20th anniversary of the Soviet cinema (1930) the stock of scientific and technical films produced in the USSR had reached a total of 4,000. Of the pictures released that year the proportion of silent and sound films was as follows: 117 sound and 54 silent scientific and technical films; 149 sound and 72 silent popular scientific films.

In this department, too, the reorganisation of 1938 had a beneficial effect. From then on, all scientific films had to be based on scenarios of literary as well as scientific merits. A number of good microfilms were made under the supervision of Professor V. Lebedee, including *Bacteria, Mosses* and *The Development of the Frog* (director Dolin), which was outstanding. Among the films on insects and animals were *Spiders* (director Vinnitzky), *Instinct in the Behaviour of Animals* (director Pavlos), which illustrated some of Darwin's theories, and, especially successful were *In the Depths of the Sea* and *The Force of Life* (director Zguridi) which developed the principles of natural selection in the life of plants and animals. Physiological films included *Circulation of the Blood* (director Karin), *Physiology and Pathology of Nervous Activity*, devoted to Academician I. Pavlov's researches, and *Disruption of the Rhythm of the Heart* (director Bazykin). A series of surgical films was made under the supervision of Academician Burdenko. Large numbers of instructional films were devoted to technical and Stakhanovite methods in industry, to the theories of metallurgy, mechanics, transport, agriculture, etc.

Among the most successful popular scientific films in addition to Zguridi's mentioned above was director Svetozarov's *Transformer of Nature*, devoted to the achievements of the botanist Michurin. Popular historical and geographical films formed part of the scientific (not documentary) programmes. They included travelogues of various rivers, the arctic regions, special films devoted to the national republics, etc.; pictures of historical relics (*Monuments of Borodino, Novgorod*); cultural films (*Pushkin's Manuscripts, The Tretiakov Gallery, Hermitage*) and many others.

The War Years

On the outbreak of war the Soviet cinema in its entirety considered itself mobilised. Its ranks were thinned by thousands joining the Forces. Those directed to continue working in their profession, reorganised on a nation-wide scale. Before the end of 1941 the Western studios were evacuated, mostly to Central Asia. In August Kiev units leap-frogged to Ashkhabad; Odessa units went to Tashkent. In October the Leningrad and Moscow units set up a joint base in Alma-Ata, the Children's Studio went to Stalinabad and the Moscow technical studios created an enlarged organisation in Novosibirsk. While the output of features was almost halved, production of documentary, technical and scientific films expanded.

It took several months before the cinema defined its role in war. At first it seemed that the arts must be sacrificed to the exigencies of war, that fiction was out of place in dealing with events of such magnitude, especially in view of the profoundly moving records of front-line cameramen and correspondents. Within three days of the Nazi invasion, the first newsreels from the front were released. Documentary took the lead, producing a veritable film chronicle of the entire war.

Soviet newsreels set a standard of uncompromising realism. The worst horrors of combat and atrocities of Nazi occupation were shown in regular issues. There were scenes of the deepest humanity, showing infants and the aged overtaken by calamity and the self-assurance and determination of the men and women in the Forces and on the home front. There were magnificent panoramas and aerial views conveying the vastness of battles and, later, the vastness of the devastation.

Speed in production was the primary consideration in the beginning, so the first documentaries were shorts. They included front-line photography by the ace cameramen Shafran and Bogdan and the first partisan reels from Eshurin, who had been landed behind the lines. Dziga Vertov edited *In the Line of Fire*. Troyanovsky recorded the exploits of the Red Air Force and the defence of Odessa. Early in 1942 came *Defeat of the Germans near Moscow*, by L. Varlamov and I. Kopalin, the first full-length documentary, which was followed by *Leningrad Fights*, by R. Karmen. V. Belyaev directed *Black Sea Marines*, a record of the 250-day defence of Sebastopol in 1942, and at the end of the year came *A Day of War*, an impressive compilation of the work of 100 cameramen along the entire front from the Arctic to the Black Sea. The documentary of the epic of Stalingrad (including Karmen's coverage) was edited by L. Varlamov early in 1943. Its inspiration seemed to match the valour of the deeds depicted: it was simple and heroic in the finest sense of the word. *Peoples Avengers* (1913, V. Belyaev) dealt with partisans. Though some of the celluloid had deteriorated in the appalling circumstances in which the reels were taken, the film gave a good idea of the magnitude and the detail of partisan operations. One of the grimmest pictures, it had moments of humour and scenes of great poignancy.

There were fewer documentaries about the home front. The best were *The Urals Forge Victory* (1943, V. Boikov), which included flash-backs of the construction of the giant Ural industries, and *Revival of Stalingrad* (1944, I. Poselsky). Special reels, such as *Pioneer, Soviet Sport, Soviet Art* (including numbers about Chekhov and the satirist Krylov) and regional newsreels appeared throughout the war.

After the change from the defensive to the offensive in 1943 the scripts of big documentaries were based on the strategic plans of campaigns. *Battle of Orel* (1943, G. Gikov, L. Stepanova), *Battle of Ukraine* (1943, supervisor A. Dovzhenko), *Sebastopol* (1944, V. Belyaev) and others, gave an idea not only of how the victories were won, but also of how they had been conceived. The greater the extent of Soviet territory liberated, the greater the monstrosities discovered. *The Khakov Trials, The Katyn Forest Atrocities*, etc., showed the remains of fearful crimes together with some of the captured criminals.

Front line cameramen maintained the highest standard throughout the war. But, early in 1944, documentary fell short of the rising standards aimed at, and the newsreels and documentary studios were reorganised. S. Gerasimov, the feature film director, was put in charge. Famous feature film producers and writers were drawn in to work on documentary, starting, not at the editing stage, as directors had often done previously, but with the planning. They co-ordinated and directed the work of the cameramen. Among the films they produced were *Berlin* (1945, Y. Raisman), *Vienna* (1945, V. Poselsky), *Victory in Ukraine* (1945,

A. Dovzhenko), and *Defeat of Japan* (1945, A. Zarkhi and J. Heifitz)—some lacked appreciation of the Allied contribution to victory. *Liberated France* (1945, S. Yutkevich), compiled from Allied newsreels, was considered outstanding. Reviewing it, Eisenstein wrote: 'At one time documentary was the leading branch of our cinema, and feature films were influenced by it. After twenty years we see the reverse process. Feature film producers have renewed contact with documentary . . . This collaboration will be fruitful to both.' In the last year of the war twenty good full-length documentaries were produced.

A number of young cameramen won fame during the war. Among them were V. Afanasiev who worked with the Red Air Force on the Southern front, contributing some of the best scenes to V. Belyaev's *Budapest* (1945); S. Shkolnikov, whose partisan pictures were included in *Peoples, Avengers* and V. Suschinsky, killed near Breslau, about whose work a documentary *A Cameraman at the Front* was made in 1946.

Documentary maintained its high standard after victory. Fine pictures were made about friendly European countries, such as I. Kopalin's *Czechoslovakia* (1946), Karmen and Troyanovsky's *Albania* (1945), and Varlamov's *Yugoslavia*. Vera Stroyeva's *Young Musicians* (1946) dealt with the work of students at the Chaikovskij Conservatoire, and S. Yutkevich's *Youth of our Country* was the 1946 multinational physical culture parade. G. Chernyak's *Road Menders* (1946) showed how military technique could be applied to reconstruction.

Production of technical and scientific films was geared almost entirely for war purposes, and developed both quantitatively and qualitatively. Total number produced in the war years was 420 films and 60 issues of the newsreel *Science & Technique*. There were instructional films on civil defence for the public, a huge number of instructional army films (*Mountain Ski Troops, Reconnaissance in Minefields, Pocket Artillery*, films on the use of weapons, tactics, etc.) and medical and surgical films, some of which were of international importance. Among the latter *Therapeutic Surgery* was outstanding. A few, such as *Medical Services on the Western Front*, were made for the broad public. Later came instructional films on reconstruction, such as *Restoration of Damaged buildings, Rebuilding Bridges*, etc. In about 1943 the production of scientific films on non-military subjects was resumed. A. Zguridi made *In the Sands of Central Asia*, a fine, popular, scientific picture about animal and insect life in the desert. A. Vinnitsky, famous for his insect films, made *Sunny Tribe*, about bees, and B. Dolin made *The Law of Great Love* which dealt with maternal love among animals, tracing the story of a family of wild foxes. A number of shorts was devoted to astronomy: *The Earth in Space, Comets, Shadow of the Moon*, etc.

68

The feature film in wartime

In the transition period, while the studios were being reorganised, production was concentrated on propaganda shorts and composite feature films, the three or four sections of which were made simultaneously by different directors in order to save time. For similar reasons the length and scope of wartime features were reduced: except for the historical films planned before the war, *Georgii Saakadze, Ivan the Terrible* and *Defence of Tsaritsin*, all made in two full-length parts, no series films were produced in wartime. Pictures were urgently wanted for immediate purposes.

The task the Soviet cinema set itself was to reveal the greatness of the epoch and its heroic people, and to inspire the nation to new deeds of courage. In this war the Soviet Union was in a unique position in that it knew subjugation and freedom at one and the same time. While huge areas of its territory were occupied and millions of its people suffered persecution and degradation which were even worse than might have been expected from the theories about Slavs in *Mein Kampf*; the rest of the nation fought on and was free to speak. The cinema, therefore, in common with the rest of the arts, endeavoured to speak on behalf of the enslaved millions as well as for those in the rear and the Forces. National consciousness and pride found particularly forceful expression. Equally marked was the stress on the connection between the heroes of this war and those of the Revolution and Socialist construction: the Red Army was defending not only their Fatherland, but also a way of life which was the fruit of their own labour and sacrifices and of those of their fathers. 'Participating in the most destructive war the world has known,' wrote Sergei Gerasimov, 'our people remain creative, for they fight for the most creative idea of all the ideas that have made history. Hence their courage in battle, their inexhaustible patience, their strength in work.'

The earliest reactions of the Soviet people to the Nazi invasion were indignation, anger and a profound sense of injustice. The outrages against those they loved, witnessed by the partisans, inspired the motto 'Death for Death'. This was the theme of several films, including *Secretary of the Regional Committee* (1942), by Ivan Pyriev and of *No Greater Love (1943)*, by Friedrich Ermler. Both were passionately sincere and factually convincing. But *No Greater Love* suffered from defects which marred many wartime features—an obvious, hastily devised script and unsubtle caricaturing of the Nazis which only made them less sinister than they were. The life of civilians in the occupied regions was shown in V. Pudovkin's *In the Name of the Fatherland* (1943), from K. Simonov's play *Russian People* which was performed by the Old Vic company in

London, Abraham Room's *Invasion* (1944) and Mark Donskoi's *Rainbow* (1944), from Wanda Wassilevska's novel. Both films had distinction. In *Rainbow* Donskoi again obtained some unforgettable performances from children, pathetic, distressed but courageous little figures who played their part in outwitting the Nazis and endured much more than their share of misery. *Rainbow* had dramatic power and its script was well wrought. Among the films devoted to the Forces were *Two Soldiers* (1943), by L. Lukov, *Submarine T-9* (1943), by A. Ivanov and Y. Raisman's *Mashenka* (1942), about a front-line nurse, and *Moscow Sky* (1941), about the fighter pilots who defended Moscow in 1941. *Two Soldiers*, probably the most successful, had a simple story about comradeship, but one of the characters was a man from Odessa, which meant that the whole film was enlivened by his witty talk and charming songs.

The hard, unspectacular labours of the people on the home front were shown in S. Gerasimov's *The Ural Front* (1944), about munition workers, and Boris *Babochmin's Native Fields* (1944), about a collective farm. The latter was *Babochkin's* (the actor who portrayed Chapaev) first venture as director. He also played a leading part in the picture, portraying a former participant in the Civil War who, though chafing to be at the front, made a job of the next best thing, supplying food to the Army.

One of the most distinguished war films was Michael Romm's *Girl 217* (1944) from an excellent screenplay by E. Gabrilovich. It dealt with the life in a German family of a Russian girl they had bought as a slave. All the characters, even the Germans, were convincing, and the terrible drama had a sense of measure and restraint which made it all the more moving. Another good film was Lev Arnstam's *Zoya* (1944), the biography of the 18-year-old heroine Zoya Kosmodemyanskaya hanged by the Germans. It sought to reveal what Soviet people died for and whence they drew their strength to endure. Through flashbacks from a scene in which the girl was being tortured the film showed her childhood, school days and youth, and also some newsreels of the big events which had impressed her. Zoya was revealed as a child moulded by the principles of the Stalin Constitution.

However, though the 1943-44 films were better than those made earlier in the war, they were not as big as their subjects. With a few exceptions, features on contemparary themes left the critics dissatisfied. They considered that, despite some fine individual performances, there was a lack of characterisation and that the spiritual sources from which typical Soviet people drew their strength remained unrevealed. In the middle of the war, as in the 1930's, a great deal was written about the need to portray the 'new man's' attitude to war. His character and his moral outlook, it was repeated again and again long before the war ended, were the foundations of victory. Towards the end of the war new emphasis was given to the need for better craftsmanship, especially screenwriting.

The historical films were up to the peacetime standard. In the Tbilisi studios Michael Chiaureli made *Georgii Saakadze*, Part. I (1942) and Part II (1943), about the seventeenth-century Georgian hero. 'The whole production', wrote the critic D. Zaslavsky, 'is in the epic style. Some of the scenes look like magnificent historical engravings. The battle scenes are admirable, not only because the huge cavalry forces covering the slopes of the mountains create a complete illusion of fierce combat, but also because the course of the battle reveals Georgii Saakadze's strategy.' The film shows something of the friendship between the Georgians and the Russians, a subject which has always been dear to Chiaureli. A. Horava's portrayal of the fiery, brilliantly intelligent Saakadze was considered a fine achievement.

Amo Bek-Nazarov made *David Bek* (Erevan, 1944) an historical picture in the romantic style of a legend, about the Armenian national leader who, with the help of Peter I of Russia, freed Armenia from the oppression of a Persian Khan.

Sergei Eisenstein's *Ivan the Terrible*, Part I (1944), was a reinterpretation of the significance in sixteenth-century Russian history of the reign of Ivan IV. The theme was his struggle to create a unified Russian state by overcoming the prolonged and cunning opposition of the nobles. Like all Eisenstein's films, it was a monumental epic. Unlike any of his previous works, its foundation was a psychological study of the central character. The inspired acting of Nikolai Cherkasov as the czar, ably supported by S. Birman as the scheming noblewoman who led the opposition, M. Nazvanov as the traitor Kurbsky and many others, was the core of the film. The whole of Eisenstein's artistry was here applied to the creation of a cinematic tragedy. He demonstrated how a synthesis of all the elements of cinema could reveal the intellectual and emotional complexities of human experience, moulding these elements in such a way as to capture the full meaning of the force and passion of the performances. I. Spinel's designs and A. Moskvin's interior photography of the heavy grandeur of the palace, cast in the gloom of court intrigue, created a sinister background for the agonising suspicions that gave Ivan no peace and for the unceasing battle of wits and will power he had to wage against the nobles. E. Tisse's exterior photography, on the other hand, light and spacious, showed Ivan revitalised, as it were, through contact with the masses whose confidence he possessed and cherished. Sergei Prokofiev's music and the sixteenth-century dialogue, beautifully written by Eisenstein, reproduced the majestic, unhurried cadence of the epoch, harmonising perfectly one with the other and with the unified rhythm of the film. The whole production was inspired by the central idea: the progressive character of Ivan's role in Russian history. It was an example of unity of form and content.

Kutuzov (1944), by Vladimir Petrov, was devoted to the aged general, hero of the Battle of Borodino, whose unpopular strategy of retreat, scorched earth and waiting saved the Russian Army in 1812 and forced Napoleon to withdraw. This picture had beautiful performances by A. Diki in the name part and S. Zakariadze as the dashing, impetuous and fearless Prince Bagration.

The historical revolutionary films, especially the Vassiliev brothers' *Defence of Tsaritsin* (1942), about the town that was renamed Stalingrad, and L. Lukov's *Alexander Parkhomenko* (1942), about one of the first Red Army commanders, had particularly poignant associations. Set in 1918, both pictures showed an untrained Red Army fighting the same invaders as the ones the modern Red Army was struggling with in the second World War, and the self-same battlefields.

A good deal was written during the war about the need for more and better comedies, and in 1944 a comedy script competition was held in order to attract humorists into films. But hardly any worth mentioning were produced. Y. Protazanov's *Adventures in Bukhara* (1943) about the gay hero of an ancient Uzbek story who took from the rich and gave to the poor, and I. Pyriev's *6 P.M.*, a musical with a war background and verse by V. Gusev, were the most successful. There were few children's films, too, which made V. Kadochnikov's charming fairytale *Magic Seed* (1942) all the more welcome.

In his November speech in 1944 Stalin said: that 'Through their creative work the Soviet intelligentsia had made an inestimable contribution to the defeat of the enemy'. The following wartime pictures were awarded Stalin prizes of the first class: *Kutuzov, Ivan the Terrible* Part I, *Zoya, Georgii Saakadze*, Part 2, *Rainbow*, and the documentaries *Revival of Stalingrad* and *Finnish Armistice*.

Reconstruction

At the end of 1943 the Moscow and Children's film units returned to their own studios, and by the end of 1944, the year in which the Soviet cinema celebrated its 25th anniversary, the rest of the evacuated units were back in their own quarters. Their studios were damaged, some of those in the liberated areas being reduced to ruins. Reconstruction and improvised production proceeded simultaneously, all film workers, irrespective of rank, helping with the building. During the war more than

8,000 projectors and 650 cinemas were destroyed. In 1944 the number of projectors in use was about 17,000 and the number of attendances for the year was approximately 600 million. The reorganisation, which envisaged the huge expansion that would be required by the 4th Five Year Plan, was far-reaching. Various innovations were commenced which were symptomatic of a new period of transition and searching for fresh paths to progress. For instance, a Film Actors' Theatre was created in Moscow, which presents scenarios in a modified form of a 'cinema play' before they are put into production in order to give actors the opportunity to develop their roles more searchingly. In March 1946, by decree of the Supreme Soviet, the Cinema Committee was transformed into the Ministry of Cinema of the USSR with I. Bolshakov as Minister.

However, the transition year 1945 was a bad one for the feature film. Of the nineteen pictures released few were good and of these fewer still dealt with contemporary themes. Among the successful films was L. Lukov's *This Happened in the Donbas* about two generations of Komsomols in the Donetz mining district, and the affinities between them. Mark Donskoi's *Unconquered* from Gorbatov's novel had as its theme the fundamental humanity and capacity for love of the very people who learnt to hate and fight the Nazis who oppressed Ukraine. This was a well-composed picture. The best of the others dealt with the past. Among them was V. Petrov's *Innocent though Guilty* from Ostrovsky's play. Three of the year's best films came from the Central Asian studios which, though suffering from congestion during the war, had gained experience by collaborating with the Western units. They were G. Roshal's *Song of Abai*, about the nineteenth-century national poet of Kazakhstan, Rza Takhmasib's *Arshin Mal-alan*, based on an Azerbaijan operette, and N. Ganiev's *Tahir and Zuhra* from an Uzbek legend. These pictures had genuine national style and marked a step forward in the development of the national cinemas of the Central Asian republics.

Early in 1946 came Friedrich Ermler's *Turning Point* from Boris Chirskov's admirable scenario, one of the most important films in the Soviet cinema. Inspired by the battle of Stalingrad, the film is a generalisation of Stalin's strategy which determined each of the Red Army's victories. It is an intensely human study of life and work in military HQ, perhaps one of the most difficult subjects to dramatise. *Turning Point* is Ermler's finest achievement in the psychological style he has been evolving with such persistence. M. Chiaureli's *The Vow*, completed later in the year, had a remarkable success in the USSR. It dealt with the fulfilment by Stalin and the nation of the vow he made when Lenin died in 1924 to continue Lenin's work. The Five Year Plans and victory

73

were the first stages in the fulfilment of the vow. The film is remarkable for M. Gelovani's portrayal of Stalin. Gelovani achieved something of a real characterisation here, something more than the 'external imitation' of his earlier performances in the same role. Otherwise the film was uneven, and made poor use of modern technique. There were a few other good films, such as V. Braun's *Far Voyage* from Stanyukovich's last-century sea stories and A Ivanov's *Sons* about the Nazi occupation of Latvia, but on the whole 1946 was not an improvement on the previous year.

For several months criticism in the Press of bad tendencies in the cinema and other arts had been growing in volume and severity, and in the early summer the storm broke. Kozintzev and Trauberg's *Simple People* about the evacuation of a Leningrad factory to Central Asia was denounced as an untrue and frivolous interpretation of Soviet people in war. Eisenstein's *Ivan the Terrible*, Part 2, was criticised for an overemphasis on court intrigue and a failure to reveal the epoch as a whole. Pudovkin's *Admiral Nakhimov*, about the hero who was killed in the Crimean War, was disapproved of because of an overstress on festive society scenes and an inadequate depiction of the Admiral's military exploits. In September came the ban of the Central Committee of the Bolshevik Party on L. Lukov's *Great Life*, Part 2, about the restoration of the Donbas, on the grounds of the film's ideological and artistic shortcomings. *Simple People, Ivan the Terrible*, Part 2, were also banned and *Admiral Nakhimov* had to be revised before it was released early in current film schedule by reducing the number of films on historical and classical subjects and increasing the number of those on contemporary themes, which were assigned to the best writers and directors.

From the wide publicity given to these events and to the numerous conferences in all departments of the cinema, it would appear that the root of the trouble was war weariness: in seeking a more 'entertaining' form of presentation, film-makers lost sight of ideology, others resorted to past history because it is easier than the creation of original works about the present time. Three dominant themes recurring in the criticism indicate the reasons why importance was attached to checking the slack tendencies forthwith: firstly, the influence of the arts on youth and the moulding of its mentality; secondly, their role as a stimulus in the reconstruction effort and the new Five Year Plan, and, finally, their international aspect and the responsibility of artists in presenting a true picture of Soviet life to the world.

Fourth Five Year Plan

In the film section of the Five Year Plan 1946-1950, the ideological aims were reaffirmed by I. Bolshakov in terms similar to those which defined Socialist realism since its beginnings. There were, of course, some more particular tasks arising out of the needs of the times. First duty was to interpret the problems of the Five Year Plan. Classics and history were of great value, but they were required only in a reasonable proportion. Films revealing the honour and poetry of labour, the diligence and inventiveness of the Soviet people, like the finest pictures of the early Five Year plans, were needed again. The Minister made many references to points in Stalin's election speech of February 1946 which must be brought out in films: victory was not only an economic and military achievement but also a victory for Soviet ideology; science was of supreme importance—here, wrote Bolshakov, the cinema could contribute by dedicating pictures to great scientists like Lomonosov, Mendeleev and Pavlov similar to *World in Blossom*, A. Dovzhenko's screenplay about the botanist Michurin (regarded by critics as outstanding) which Dovzhenko began producing as a colour film in 1946; the strength of Soviet democracy and its multi-national system—in this connection Bolshakov urged the further development of the cinemas of the national republics, noting the progress of the Central Asian units and making special reference to the creation of national cinemas in the Baltic republics (in the summer of 1946 the Film Ministry of Latvia had already been instituted and film production commenced). The time had come for films with an historical approach to the great moments of the war; more pictures like *Turning Point* were needed, also films about war heroes. Pictures dedicated to family life and to motherhood must be made, and better films for children. The difficulties of producing comedies must at last be overcome. The Minister noted the good work of the Artistic Council of the Film Ministry since its creation in raising the standard of production of features, which had deteriorated during the war. He laid stress on the importance of screenwriting as the foundation of cinema. In order to give writers every facility, scenario departments had recently been re-established in the film studios, working concurrently with the Central Script Studio. (Broad themes, like those of the latter 1930's, again became a characteristic feature of the script schedules of 1946-47.) Documentary must continue its fine work, and the expansion of scientific film production had become more than ever important. (Since the end of the war scientific film festivals, lectures, etc., have been held with increasing frequency.)

By the end of the Five Year Plan production should average 80 to 100 features a year. Of these the enlarged Moscow studios with their base in Odessa will make 40. New studios are to be built in Minsk, Riga, Tallin, Vilnus and Baku. The rest, including documentary and scientific studios, will be renovated and enlarged. Production of equipment is to be expanded and scientific research into new techniques intensified, especially in relation to colour cinema. (In 1946 R. Novitsky perfected a plexiglass and dualumin installation for showing films in daylight, outdoors or indoors; an earlier model had already been used in the Central Park of the Red Army in 1935.) The number of projectors should be raised to 46,000. During the period of the plan the Film Institute will train over 400 high-grade specialists, such as directors, actors, etc., a new faculty for make-up artists will be created and the historians and critics faculties will train 40 new specialists. In addition 400 actors will be trained at the institutes attached to the studios. The Leningrad and Kiev Technical Institutes will train over 1,000 engineers and other institutes will train 1,500 technicians. By the end of the Five Year Plan the film industry should employ 178,000 workers of all grades.

Colour

Few colour films were made in the USSR before the war. N. Ekk's *Nightingale* and B. Barnet's *Blue Sea*, the first full-length pictures made in a two-colour system, appeared in 1936. They were experimental. The same system, perfected, was used for a number of children's films, among which *Little Humpback Horse* was outstanding. *Sorochinsk Fair* made by N. Ekk in Kiev in 1939, was a further development of the system. Research into colour photography continued during the war, and in 1944 Igor Savchenko completed the first Soviet three-colour system film *Ivan Nikulin, Russian Sailor*, which was a success. Savchenko chose a story of characters, not one with any particular 'colourful' background, and endeavoured to use colour not for its own sake but solely for the purpose of interpreting the theme more dramatically. Several scientific pictures, newsreels, including *Trophies of War*, and documentaries, such as the 1945 Physical Culture Parade, were made in colour. The latter was outstanding for its delicacy and colour perspective. In 1946 A. Ptushko, who made the remarkable puppet films *New Gulliver* (1935) and *Golden Key* (1939) produced *Stone Flower* in Prague in the captured German Agfa system. It was a fantasy based on Ural folklore and designed from drawings made in the Urals in the style of the art of the region. It promised well for the Soviet colour film. *The Victory Parade in Moscow* was among the documentaries successfully filmed by the same combined system. An enormous amount was written in 1946-47 about the importance of colour, and among the films put into production during that time were S. Yutkevich's *Light over Russia*, about electrification, and I. Pyriev's *Tale of Siberia*.

Cartoons

In August 1946 the Moscow Cartoon studio celebrated its tenth anniversary. In ten years it had produced more than 100 cartoons, including *The Tale of Czar Sultan* and *Tomtit*. Nearly all of these were intended for children and were based on folklore, comedies and fables. During the war some anti-Fascist cartoons were made. When, in 1945, the children's cartoons *Sindbad* and *The Stolen Sun* were released, critics called for a wider showing of animated cartoons because they would entertain the general public no less than children. A full-length colour cartoon in five parts, based on Gogol's *Lost Charter*, was also well received. In the same year the studio moved into a newly equipped building where, by the end of the Five Year Plan, 24 film parts (about five full-length films) will be made annually. Modern Soviet themes predominated in the new schedule. There is also a cartoon studio in Tbilisi, which released a successful colour cartoon, *Three Comrades*, in 1946.

Stereoscopic cinema

In 1936 Semen Ivanov, son of a shoemaker, began practical research on the stereoscopic invention he had already worked out in theory. He was a Komsomol in his early twenties, passionately interested in art, but disheartened by the flatness of painting. Two years later he was able to demonstrate his first imperfect stereoscopic film screen for showing films without the spectator having to wear special spectacles. In 1940 his stereoscopic screen, covered by a grid of 36,000 copper wires radiating in three directions, was installed in the cinema 'Moskva' in Moscow. The three-dimensional effect was created by simultaneously projecting onto it two films depicting the same scenes from different angles. Before the war half a million Muscovites saw the short picture *Film Concert*. It gave one the illusion that the action on the screen was taking place in the auditorium—transparent fish came swimming through the air towards one, it seemed that one could touch the characters as they approached.

On the outbreak of war, Ivanov went to the front, putting his stereoscopic experience to good use in reconnaissance. By 1942 work on stereoscopic films was resumed and the next year Ivanov demonstrated a better, simpler and less heavy screen. It is made of myriads of optical lenses designed to split the rays of light. Arrangements were made to put it into mass production, a stereoscopic film studio was founded in 1945 and the producer, A. Andrievsky, began work on the first full-length colour stereoscopic film, *Robinson Crusoe*. The name part is taken by P. Kadochnikov whose former roles include the half-imbecile pretender to the succession in *Ivan the Terrible*. A comedy, *Machine No. 22-12*, also went into production.

During the war the cameraman D. Surenski and A. Ulyantzev made a stereoscopic documentary about children, and another, *In the Steps of the Enemy,* about war damage in historical places. V. Volodarski produced a stereoscopic film of the physical culture parade of 1945. By the end of 1946 the stereoscopic studio had enough trained specialists to produce three to four full-length films yearly.

Early in 1947 the new screen, measuring 9 square metres, was installed in a Moscow cinema, and the recently completed *Robinson Crusoe* presented to the public. It was a new pioneering triumph for the Soviet cinema.

Throughout its history of successes and failures, the Soviet cinema has maintained an unbroken, in some ways, unequalled record of purposeful striving for progress. It has made many contributions to the development of cinema as an art that are of permanent value. The inspiring programme of the 4th Five Year Plan foreshadows new departures and new achievements of international significance.

PLATES

THE BATTLESHIP POTEMKIN
1925 S. M. Eisenstein

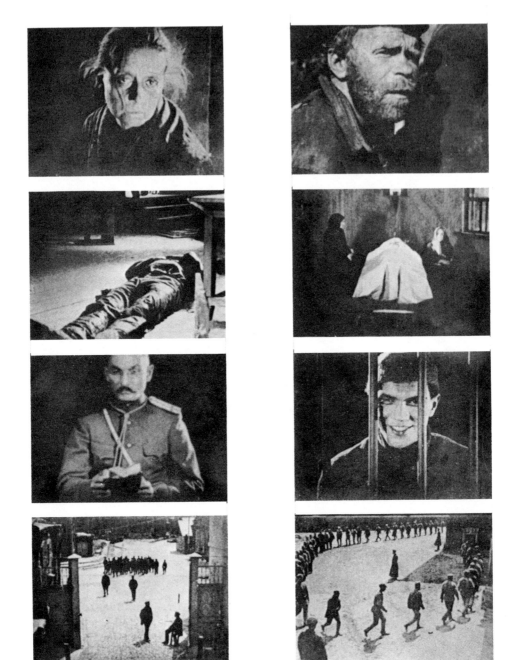

MOTHER
1926 V. I. Pudovkin

END OF ST. PETERSBURG
1927
V. I. Pudovkin

ARSENAL
1929
A. Dovzhenko

TURKSIB
1928 V. Turin

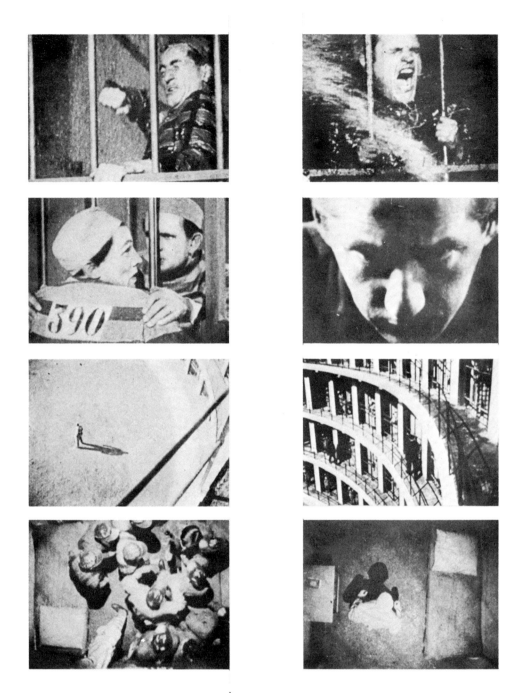

THE GHOST THAT NEVER RETURNS
1929 Alexander Room

OCTOBER (The Ten Days that Shook the World)
1928 S. M. Eisenstein

OCTOBER

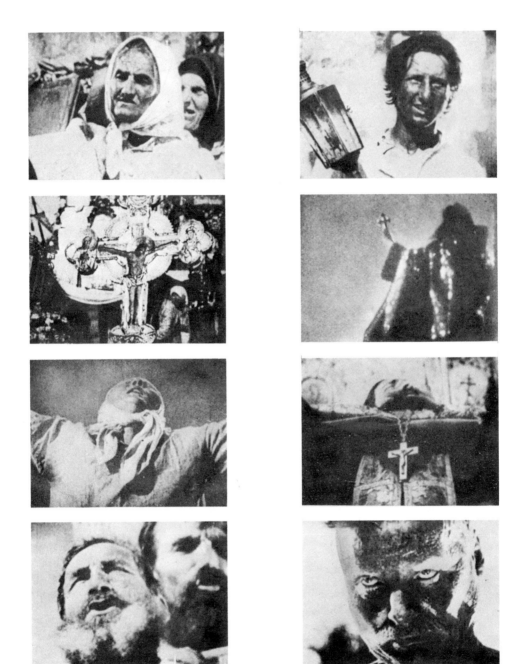

THE GENERAL LINE
1929 S. M. Eisenstein

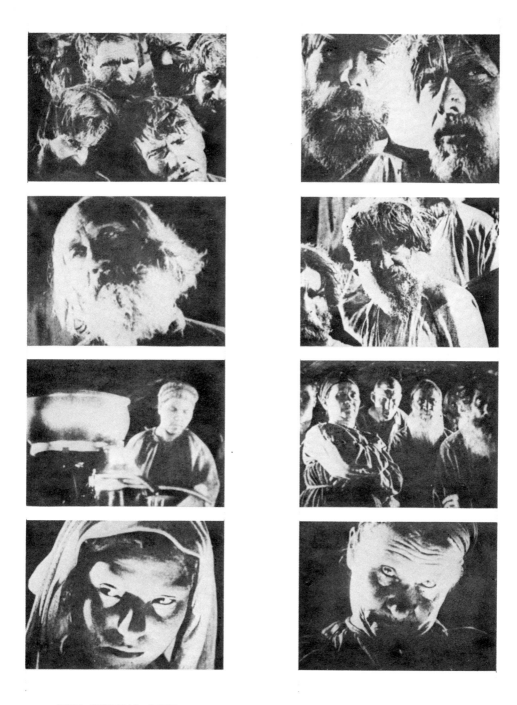

THE GENERAL LINE

FRAGMENT OF AN EMPIRE
1929
F. Ermler

EARTH
1930
A. Dovzhenko

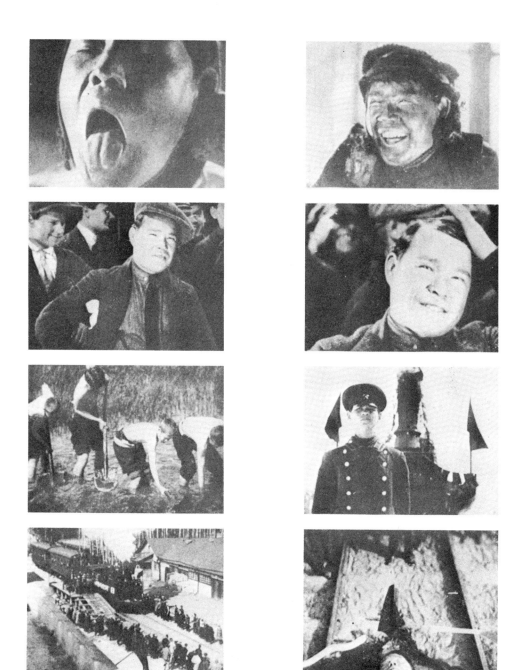

THE ROAD TO LIFE
1931 N. Ekk

DESERTER
1933
V. I. Pudovkin

DESERTER

STORM
1934
V. Petrov

JAZZ COMEDY
1934
G. V. Alexandrov

THE CIRCUS
1936
G. V. Alexandrov

THE CIRCUS

THE NEW GULLIVER
1935
A. Ptushko

THE NEW GULLIVER

THE NEW GULLIVER

CHAPAYEV
1934
G. & S. Vassiliev

CHAPAYEV

WE FROM KRONSTADT
1936
E. Dzigan and Vishnevsky

SEVEN BRAVE MEN
1936
S. Gerasimov

SEVEN BRAVE MEN

SEVEN BRAVE MEN

THE BALTIC DEPUTY
1937
A. Zharkhi and Heifitz

THE BALTIC DEPUTY

THE BALTIC DEPUTY

THE THIRTEEN
1937
M. Romm

THE THIRTEEN

LONE WHITE SAIL
1937
V. Legoshin

LENIN IN OCTOBER
1937
M. Romm

LENIN IN OCTOBER

LENIN IN 1918
1939
M. Romm

GREAT CITIZEN
1938
F. Ermler

GREAT CITIZEN

GREAT CITIZEN

THE CHILDHOOD OF MAXIM GORKI
1938
M. Donskoi

THE CHILDHOOD OF MAXIM GORKI

MY UNIVERSITIES
1940
M. Donskoi

PETER THE GREAT
Part I
1937
V. Petrov

PETER THE GREAT
Part II
V. Petrov

PETER THE GREAT
Part II

ALEXANDER NEVSKY
1938
S. M. Eisenstein

ALEXANDER NEVSKY

ALEXANDER NEVSKY

MEMBER OF THE GOVERNMENT
American version was called
THE GREAT BEGINNING
1939
Alexander Zharkhi and Josef Heifitz

MEMBER OF THE GOVERNMENT

PROFESSOR MAMLOCK
1938
A. Minkin

SHORS
1939
A. Dovzhenko

SHORS

SHORS

BOGDAN KHMELNITZKI
1941
I. Savchenko

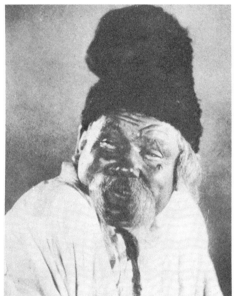

BOGDAN KHMELNITZKI

BOGDAN KHMELNITZKI

GENERAL SUVOROV
1940
V. Pudovkin

GENERAL SUVOROV

GENERAL SUVOROV

TRACTOR DRIVERS
1939
I. Pyryev

TRACTOR DRIVERS

JACOB SVERDLOV
1940
S. Yutkevich

MASQUERADE
1941
Sergei Gerasimov

MASQUERADE

LERMONTOV
1943
A. Gendelstein

THE MAGIC SEED
1942
Supervised by
S. M. Eisenstein

ADVENTURE IN BUKHARA
1943
J. Protazanov

MARRIAGE
1944
V. Petrov

GEORGII SAAKADZE
Part I
1942
M. Chiaureli

GEORGII SAAKADZE

GEORGII SAAKADZE

THE DEFENCE OF TZARITZIN
1942
G. & S. Vassiliev

THE DEFENCE OF TZARITZIN

THE DEFENCE OF TZARITZIN

SECRETARY OF THE
DISTRICT COMMITTEE
1942
I. Pyriev

SECRETARY OF THE
DISTRICT COMMITTEE

SECRETARY OF THE
DISTRICT COMMITTEE

GIRL 217
1944
Michael Romm

GIRL 217

GIRL 217

THE RAINBOW
1944
M. Donskoi

THE RAINBOW

THE RAINBOW

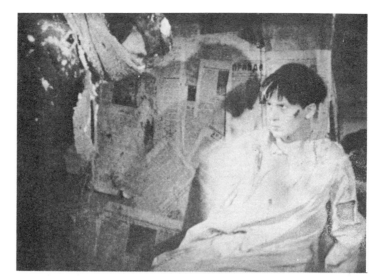

ZOYA
1944
L. Arnstam

ZOYA

ZOYA

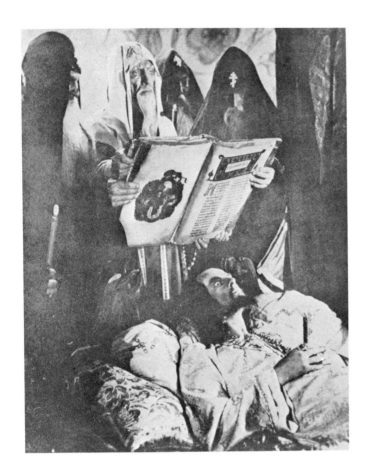

IVAN THE TERRIBLE
Part I
1944
S. M. Eisenstein

IVAN THE TERRIBLE
Part I
1944
S. M. Eisenstein

UNCONQUERED
1945
M. Donskoi

UNCONQUERED

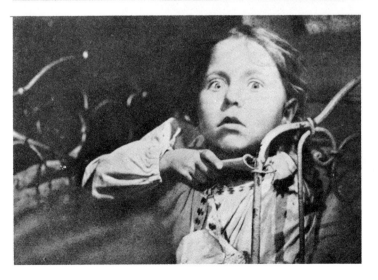

UNCONQUERED

SONG OF ABAI
1945
G. Roshal

SONG OF ABAI

SONG OF ABAI

THE TURNING POINT
1946
F. Ermler

THE TURNING POINT

ADMIRAL NAKHIMOV
1946
V. I. Pudovkin

THE VOW
1946
M. Chiaureli

THE VOW

THE VOW

ZIGMUND KOLOSOVSKY
1946
L. S. Navrocki

ZIGMUND KOLOSOVSKY

ZIGMUND KOLOSOVSKY

THE STONE FLOWER
1946
A. Ptusko

ELEPHANT AND THE
SKIPPING ROPE
1946
I. Frez

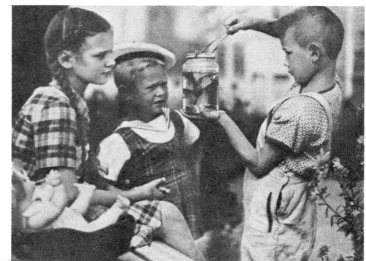

THE FIFTEEN-YEAR-OLD CAPTAIN
1946
V. Zhuravlev

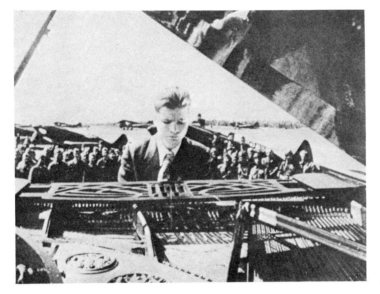

ONE DAY OF WAR
1942
Central Newsreel Studios

THE KHARKOV TRIAL
(Justice is Coming)
1945

TADJIKISTAN
1946
L. Stepanova

YUGOSLAVIA
1946
L. Varlamov

YUGOSLAVIA

YUGOSLAVIA

GLINKA   L. Arnstam. 1947

GLINKA

APPENDIX A

A Synopsis of Eisenstein's Film *October*

Produced by Sovkino, Moscow. 9,774 feet. Scenario and Direction by S. M. Eisenstein and Gregori Alexandrov. Photography by Edward Tisse. The part of Lenin played by Nikandov, that of Kerensky by N. Popov. (*October* is assembled in ten episodes.[1])

I. A statue of the czar; workers run to it, climb it bearing ropes, led by a woman.[2] As they tie the ropes, a mass of soldiers raise their rifles in the air, a mass of labourers their scythes—a title *February 1917*—and the limbs of the statue break off in slow motion, the whole statue toppling over and over again. The bourgeoisie rejoice, the Church celebrates the rise of the Provisional Government (a rain of smoky close-ups) and at the front Russian fraternises with German, exchanging food, hats, speeches, laughs, applause. But the Government decides to honour the czarist commitments with their allies, and at the front explosions send the friends back into their trenches to shoot each other down. Tanks advance and war factories produce more armaments. Queues for bread, rations cut, women in the snow—*Hunger and War* as before. *April 3rd*, searchlights play over men outside *the Finland Terminus*, waiting for *HIM*. He hurries from the station, climbs on an armoured car, seizes a flag, *LENIN!* He greets the crowd with *Down with the Provisional Government. Long live the Socialist Revolution.*

II. *Not bread—not land.* In July a procession of workers with banners passes through Petrograd: *Down with the Capitalist Ministers.* Armed sailors from Kronstadt march with them. Trotsky halts the armed men, begs them to march peacefully. They put aside their rifles. In the great square near the Government offices and the capitalist newspaper buildings two processions meet and unite. Suddenly machine-guns open fire from above (shots intercut in fractions of a split second, jolting

---

[1] Until recently most cinemas or travelling showmen in Russia were equipped with only one film projector. Therefore each reel of film was designed as an entity and the pauses for changing the reels provided a dramatic interval in the structure of the film also.

[2] It is women who turn against the White Guards on the Odessa Steps in *Potemkin* and it is a woman who leads the progressive collective movement against the reactionary kulak farmers in *Old and New*. Women play an emphatic part for and against the revolution in *October*.

129

the eye), the crowds run for shelter in all directions. A young man bearing a banner runs to the river bank to hide his burden, disturbs a loving couple, an officer and a young woman. They attack him mercilessly as a Bolshevik, other bourgeois women joining in, brutally stabbing, kicking, mutilating. A horse drawing a cab and a young woman are fleeing across a bridge. A civil servant telephones for the river bridges to be raised to cut off the workers' quarters from the centre of the city. Horse and woman are shot down at middle joint of the bridge, which begins to open. The woman's hair falls into the gap. The horse dangles over the gap, sustained by the weight of the cab on the rising edge of the bridge. Bourgeois citizens shower copies of the Bolshevik newspaper *Pravda* (Truth) into the river. Banners from the procession are thrown into the river. The white horse falls from the steep bridge end into the water. Banners, newspapers sink under the surface. The bridge tilts higher, cab and woman slither down the steep slope of the bridge onto the permanent roadway. (Tremendous agitated tempo built up from the first scenes of the procession. Now a sudden change to slowness.) A column of unarmed troops march slowly into the city, the First Machine-Gun Corps disarmed for solidarity with the Bolsheviks.

Traitors. The Bolshevik headquarters wrecked by the bourgeoisie.

III. Kerensky enters the Winter Palace, climbs the grand staircase, greets each of the row of flunkeys—*What a democrat!*—and pauses at the doorway to the state apartments. A bronze peacock swings slowly round, opening its plumes, the flunkeys grin, and the double doors open (emphasis gained by repeating the actions in shot after shot). Kerensky slowly enters the apartments. Sailors, soldiers, workers, listless in prison: *Bolsheviks.* Hiding in the marshes among the mists, *Lenin.* In the Winter Palace in the private apartments of the imperial family, Kerensky. The monogram A for Alexander everywhere, even on the imperial chamber pots. In the library Kerensky signs an order, re-introducing the death penalty. He explores further, examines a statue of Napoleon, toy soldiers, a four-way decanter capped with a crown. As he replaces the crown on the decanter, steam whistles are blown. *The revolution is in danger. Kornilov* is advancing against Petrograd. All to the defence. *For God and Country. For God:* a succession of religious images, Christian, Hindu, Buddhist and so to primitive tribal deities and representations of mumbo-jumbo. *For Country:* crates of orders and decorations, gold lace and ribbons. *Hurrah!* The statue of the czar reintegrates and rocks onto its pedestal. Idols and medals. Censers swing, fuming, priests make holy gestures, Kornilov sits on his horse, the statue of Napoleon stands erect on its pedestal, Kerensky wilts, two statues of Napoleon appear. *Two*

130

Bonapartes. Tanks advance, Kornilov threatens, Kerensky flings himself onto a pile of cushions, a tank flings itself over a ditch.

IV. Kornilov advances *with the Wild Division* with English tanks and armoured cars, while Kerensky lies face downwards, kicking the cushions. *The Government is helpless.* Workers break into the arsenals, seize weapons, release their fellow workers from prison, *Betrayers!*—and distribute arms. *The Petersburg* Proletariat—*takes over the defence.* The defence headquarters are at the Smolny Institute, banners, bundles of propaganda leaflets, arms and ammunition, lorries of fighters, uprooting of railway lines, of points. Night and a train at a standstill—the Wild Division of Cossacks draw their daggers. Three civilians, *Bolsheviks,* approach the sentry on the train, hand out leaflets to the Cossacks, *telling in their native tongues of Bread, Peace, Land, Brotherhood.* The Cossacks sheathe their weapons, laugh, fraternise, dance while Kerensky still lies kicking those cushions. (The fast dance climax here is over-played and held too long.) While they dance, *General Kornilov* is arrested.

V. *Proletariat! Learn to use arms*—musketry training of civilians, drilling, marching, *ready to fight.* The Bolshevik Central Committee decide on a rising against the Government, not before, not after, but on the day set for the second Soviet Congress, October 25th. The cruiser *Aurora* lies in the river. The Government once more raises the bridges, cutting off the workers from the centre of the city. Sailors from the *Aurora* land, drive away cadet guards, lower and guard the bridges, across which trams begin to run again. Kerensky telephones for Cossacks, but none stir. Pickets of sailors on duty. Kerensky drives off in a U.S. staff car to Gatchin to *raise a following and crush the rebellion.* Cadets march in to guard the Winter Palace, followed by the Women's Shock Brigade of Death. A member of the Government addresses them. Those off duty go to rest, some of the women settle down on the imperial billiard table. Outside preparations are being made for defence.

VI. At the call of the Military Revolutionary Committee men and vehicles move out to take up positions for the attack. Mensheviks (the more moderate wing of the Soviet) arrive for the Congress, ratfaced intellectuals, nearly all wearing pince-nez. A stranger arrives, Lenin, his face hidden in a muffler. Delegates come from all over the country. After dark the Congress assembles. In the Winter Palace the ministers sit around a table, at its head an empty chair. The bonnet of Kerensky's car bears its U.S. flag. At Smolny the Congress opens with Mensheviks in charge. They support the Provisional Government, while the militant Bolsheviks continue planning the attack on their maps. The Mensheviks

131

demand support against the Bolsheviks (the more extreme group). *The Bolsheviks will bring ruin.* But when the crowded Congress votes, the Bolsheviks are elected and the Mensheviks are forced to leave the rostrum.

VII.   The people's army takes up position. Orders are telephoned. Movement in the streets. (There is an inordinate amount of rushing about, indoors and out.) *The Red Army encloses the Winter Palace in a ring of steel.* The Congress continues. A demand for surrender to avoid bloodshed is written and carried to the Winter Palace by messengers with a white flag. A woman soldier receives it and passes it into the building. Waiting. Ministers sleeping, one running his fingers over the strings of a harp engraved on a glass partition. Sailors round a fire. Proletarian fighters snipe at the statues on the building. *The emotion of the moment is too great for some.* A faded woman soldier examines a statue of two lovers by Rodin. Her eyes fill with tears. 11 p.m. 11.30 p.m.

VIII.   *Agitators from the Smolny penetrate into the Winter Palace.* They enter through cellars, past electric cables, up stairways, along elaborate galleries with chandeliers. In the kitchens cooks and waiters are preparing meals for the ministers as usual. The agitators reach the Cossacks in the inner couryard and begin talking to them. An officer insults a sentry—*Son of a bitch*—the statue of a mother teaching her child to walk, a woman soldier at bayonet practice. A fat, bespectacled minister addresses cadets, emphasising no surrender. Sailors watch from gallery. At the Congress Mensheviks heckle Bolsheviks. Delegates from the 12th Army declare their solidarity. A soldier rushes in, shouts: *Comrades, the Cycle Corps is with us.* Cycle wheels fill the screen. The sailor in the gallery of the Winter Palace throws a grenade among the cadets. The Cossack artillery gallops out of the Palace, deserting the Government. But *still no answer* to the ultimatum.

IX.   A Menshevik addresses the Congress, appealing for a solution by peaceful, non-violent methods. Three women play on harps. The Menshevik continues his appeal, while in the Winter Palace the Provisional Government procrastinates and a man plays a balalaika. The envoys with the white flag return from the Palace and firing begins. Sculpture on the façade is shattered, chandeliers within the building vibrate. Speakers at the Congress demand action, for *Bread, land, peace.* The cruiser *Aurora* opens fire on the Winter Palace. The Mayor of Petrograd at the head of the bourgeois Committee of Salvation crosses a bridge to parley with the workers and is held up by pickets of sailors. In the cabinet room the chairs of the ministers round the table are occupied

132

by empty hats and suits of clothes. While the Mensheviks are still pro-
testing, midnight strikes and the Bolsheviks set the people's army on to
attack the Winter Palace. The attack begins (action speeded up in the
cameras). The people break into the wine cellars.

X.   The people pour up through the palace into the state apartments,
rip up the bedding, smash the furniture, tip over the crates of medals,
drive out the women soldiers, who surrender with the other troops. A
child climbs onto the imperial throne. The Ministers are arrested in
their council room. By 2 a.m. (the clock showing the comparative times
in all the capitals of the world) the Provisional Government is over-
thrown and Lenin announces the news to the cheering Congress.

APPENDIX B

Old and New

Produced by Sovkino, Moscow, 1928 to 1929. 8,100 feet.
Scenario and direction by S. M. Eisenstein and Gregori Alexandrov.
Photographed by Edward Tisse.

I. In a wide undulating landscape peasants are asleep in a small squalid hut. At dawn they rise. The father is dead. The sons set to work to divide the inheritance, the father's land, fencing off each son's share. It is spring. Marfa Lapkina begs from a *kulak* family, who refuse her food or money. The *kulaks* have horses to pull their ploughs. The poor use their cow, or themselves to drag their ploughs. Marfa Lapkina's cow throws a fit. She stops ploughing, determined to persuade her neighbours to combine with her.

II. In the village an agricultural officer addresses a meeting proposing that the peasants combine in a Co-operative Society to pool their land in a collective farm. Only Marfa Lapkina is enthusiastic. She persuades others to join her. There is a drought. The local priests and villagers form a religious procession carrying crosses and ikons through the fields, marching, kneeling, singing, praying for rain. Kneelers prostrate themselves, the procession flowing past and over them. Cripples drag themselves fervently among the throng over the dry earth, past the thirsty sheep and cattle. Clouds are blown across the sun. The worshippers prostrate themselves in suspense. The clouds pass away. The sun beats down on the sweating, despairing peasants. The Co-operative Society's first investment is a cream separator. The agricultural officer proudly snatches the cover off the gleaming machine, pours in the milk, and sets the mechanics in motion as the peasants watch, breathless, excited, sceptical, or pessimistic. The tempo becomes more staccato and then grows faster as they watch and wait until the cream begins to drip from the spout into the bucket. Then flashing, gleaming, twinkling, the screen is dancing with joyful images of the proud purchasers and their new possession.

III. Marfa finds members of the Co-operative breaking into the Society's cash box and taking the money for themselves. When she tries to stop them, they beat her. The agricultural officer comes, browbeats

134

them and persuades them to return all the money, which they have been collectively saving to buy a bull for breeding. That night Marfa dreams of the bull and of the fertility of nature, of rain clouds, flowing milk, of piggeries and incubation. Awake, she finds all these things at the Central Co-operative of the province, which she visits to buy the young bull, Tommy. Back on the farm they celebrate the marriage of Tommy and the finest cow of the herd. They garland the cow in the field and the bull in the barn. Then they open the doors of the barn and the bull makes for the cow, gathering speed as it approaches. Explosions fill the screen.

IV. It is high summer and the peasants cut the hay with scythes, the young racing the old. A mowing machine overtakes them all. In the autumn their application to buy a tractor is turned down. Red tape and rubber stamps. They reap their corn by hand, the wind blusters the corn and the clothes of the reapers, bringing rain which drenches them. More official forms, more rubber stamps, more red tape. Marfa travels by road and rail to Kharkov, to the tractor factory. She is awed by the clusters of tall new government buildings.

V. In Marfa's absence the *kulaks*, intent on sabotaging the Co-operative, break into the barn at night and poison Tommy, the bull. Marfa arrives at the tractor factory, insults the conventional office workers, quotes Lenin to them. This galvanises them into activity. They agree to give the co-operative credit for a tractor to be delivered immediately. On the farm members of the Society fail to revive the dying bull with quack remedies. Kulaks watch; turkeys strut about, gobbling. Marfa returns in the evening, successful and happy, carrying two toy balloons. She finds the dead bull. The balloons float away. She sinks to the ground in grief. A young bull calf, son of Tommy, comes and stands above her. Marfa laughs through her tears.

VI. It is a holiday. The tractor has arrived in the charge of a mechanic decked out in a starched collar, cuffs, and shirt front, and a leather helmet with a visor. The local band plays. The villagers watch the mechanic start the engine. The noise excites the animals. Horses bolt with their carts, geese scatter. The tractor moves and stops. The band stops playing. Something is wrong. The villagers disperse. The mechanic tears off his cuffs and collar and uses his shirt front to clean the engine. Marfa coyly allows him to tear a piece off her petticoat for the same purpose. The disgusted peasants retire to the inn, leaving their carts and horses unattended. The mechanic repairs the engine. He helps Marfa climb aboard, and they drive to the inn. Here they tie all the

135

carts together and tow them away over the landscape. The peasants run out of the inn alarmed, jump on their horses and chase the train of carts. The band plays. The tractor breaks through the fences around individual farms. Dozens of tractors drive out of the factory over the landscape, ploughing, circling, advancing in mass formation.

Finale: A boy and girl on a haycart meet a figure in goggles and a leather helmet, driving a tractor. The goggled one is Marfa. Her story is summarised in recapitulation. The boy leaves his girl in the haycart and embraces Marfa.

The Arno Press Cinema Program

THE LITERATURE OF CINEMA

Series I & II

American Academy of Political and Social Science. **The Motion Picture in Its Economic and Social Aspects,** edited by Clyde L. King. **The Motion Picture Industry,** edited by Gordon S. Watkins. *The Annals,* November, 1926/1927.

Agate, James. **Around Cinemas.** 1946.

Agate, James. **Around Cinemas.** (Second Series). 1948.

Balcon, Michael, Ernest Lindgren, Forsyth Hardy and Roger Manvell. **Twenty Years of British Film, 1925-1945.** 1947.

Bardèche, Maurice and Robert Brasillach. **The History of Motion Pictures,** edited by Iris Barry. 1938.

Benoit-Levy, Jean. **The Art of the Motion Picture.** 1946.

Blumer, Herbert. **Movies and Conduct.** 1933.

Blumer, Herbert and Philip M. Hauser. **Movies, Delinquency, and Crime.** 1933.

Buckle, Gerard Fort. **The Mind and the Film.** 1926.

Carter, Huntly. **The New Spirit in the Cinema.** 1930.

Carter, Huntly. **The New Spirit in the Russian Theatre, 1917-1928.** 1929.

Carter, Huntly. **The New Theatre and Cinema of Soviet Russia.** 1924.

Charters, W. W. **Motion Pictures and Youth.** 1933.

Cinema Commission of Inquiry. **The Cinema: Its Present Position and Future Possibilities.** 1917.

Dale, Edgar. **The Content of Motion Pictures.** 1935.

Dale, Edgar. **How to Appreciate Motion Pictures.** 1937.

Dale, Edgar. **Children's Attendance at Motion Pictures.** Dysinger, Wendell S. and Christian A. Ruckmick. **The Emotional Responses of Children to the Motion Picture Situation.** 1935.

Dale, Edgar, Fannie W. Dunn, Charles F. Hoban, Jr., and Etta Schneider. **Motion Pictures in Education: A Summary of the Literature.** 1938.

Davy, Charles. **Footnotes to the Film.** 1938.

Dickinson, Thorold and Catherine De la Roche. **Soviet Cinema.** 1948.

Dickson, W. K. L., and Antonia Dickson. **History of the Kinetograph, Kinetoscope and Kinetophonograph.** 1895.

Forman, Henry James. **Our Movie Made Children.** 1935.

Freeburg, Victor Oscar. **The Art of Photoplay Making.** 1918.

Freeburg, Victor Oscar. **Pictorial Beauty on the Screen.** 1923.

Hall, Hal, editor. **Cinematographic Annual,** 2 vols. 1930/1931.

Hampton, Benjamin B. **A History of the Movies.** 1931.

Hardy, Forsyth. **Scandinavian Film.** 1952.

Hepworth, Cecil M. **Animated Photography: The A B C of the Cinematograph.** 1900.

Hoban, Charles F., Jr., and Edward B. Van Ormer. **Instructional Film Research 1918-1950.** 1950.

Holaday, Perry W. and George D. Stoddard. **Getting Ideas from the Movies.** 1933.

Hopwood, Henry V. **Living Pictures.** 1899.

Hulfish, David S. **Motion-Picture Work.** 1915.

Hunter, William. **Scrutiny of Cinema.** 1932.

Huntley, John. **British Film Music.** 1948.

Irwin, Will. **The House That Shadows Built.** 1928.

Jarratt, Vernon. **The Italian Cinema.** 1951.

Jenkins, C. Francis. **Animated Pictures.** 1898.

Lang, Edith and George West. **Musical Accompaniment of Moving Pictures.** 1920.

L'Art Cinematographique, Nos. 1-8. 1926-1931.

London, Kurt. **Film Music.** 1936.

Lutz, E [dwin] G [eorge]. **The Motion-Picture Cameraman.** 1927.

Manvell, Roger. **Experiment in the Film.** 1949.

Marey, Etienne Jules. **Movement.** 1895.

Martin, Olga J. **Hollywood's Movie Commandments.** 1937.

Mayer, J. P. **Sociology of Film: Studies and Documents.** 1946. New Introduction by J. P. Mayer.

Münsterberg, Hugo. **The Photoplay: A Psychological Study.** 1916.

Nicoll, Allardyce. **Film and Theatre.** 1936.

Noble, Peter. **The Negro in Films.** 1949.

Peters, Charles C. **Motion Pictures and Standards of Morality.** 1933.

Peterson, Ruth C. and L. L. Thurstone. **Motion Pictures and the Social Attitudes of Children.** Shuttleworth, Frank K. and Mark A. May. **The Social Conduct and Attitudes of Movie Fans.** 1933.

Phillips, Henry Albert. **The Photodrama.** 1914.

Photoplay Research Society. **Opportunities in the Motion Picture Industry.** 1922.

Rapée, Erno. **Encyclopaedia of Music for Pictures.** 1925.

Rapée, Erno. **Motion Picture Moods for Pianists and Organists.** 1924.

Renshaw, Samuel, Vernon L. Miller and Dorothy P. Marquis. **Children's Sleep.** 1933.

Rosten, Leo C. **Hollywood: The Movie Colony, The Movie Makers.** 1941.

Sadoul, Georges. **French Film.** 1953.

Screen Monographs I, 1923-1937. 1970.

Screen Monographs II, 1915-1930. 1970.

Sinclair, Upton. **Upton Sinclair Presents William Fox.** 1933.

Talbot, Frederick A. **Moving Pictures.** 1912.

Thorp, Margaret Farrand. **America at the Movies.** 1939.

Wollenberg, H. H. **Fifty Years of German Film.** 1948.

RELATED BOOKS AND PERIODICALS

Allister, Ray. **Friese-Greene: Close-Up of an Inventor.** 1948.

Art in Cinema: A Symposium of the Avant-Garde Film, edited by Frank Stauffacher. 1947.

The Art of Cinema: Selected Essays. New Foreword by George Amberg. 1971.

Balázs, Béla. **Theory of the Film.** 1952.

Barry, Iris. **Let's Go to the Movies.** 1926.

de Beauvoir, Simone. **Brigitte Bardot and the Lolita Syndrome.** 1960.

Carrick, Edward. **Art and Design in the British Film.** 1948.

Close Up. Vols. 1-10, 1927-1933 (all published).

Cogley, John. **Report on Blacklisting. Part I: The Movies.** 1956.

Eisenstein, S. M. **Que Viva Mexico!** 1951.

Experimental Cinema. 1930-1934 (all published).

Feldman, Joseph and Harry. **Dynamics of the Film.** 1952.

Film Daily Yearbook of Motion Pictures. Microfilm, 18 reels,
    35 mm. 1918-1969.

Film Daily Yearbook of Motion Pictures. 1970.

Film Daily Yearbook of Motion Pictures. (Wid's Year Book).
    3 vols., 1918-1922.

The Film Index: A Bibliography. Vol. I: The Film as Art. 1941.

Film Society Programmes. 1925-1939 (all published).

Films: A Quarterly of Discussion and Analysis. Nos. 1-4, 1939-1940
    (all published).

Flaherty, Frances Hubbard. **The Odyssey of a Film-Maker:
    Robert Flaherty's Story.** 1960.

General Bibliography of Motion Pictures, edited by Carl Vincent,
    Riccardo Redi, and Franco Venturini. 1953.

Hendricks, Gordon. **Origins of the American Film.** 1961-1966. New
    Introduction by Gordon Hendricks.

Hound and Horn: Essays on Cinema, 1928-1934. 1971.

Huff, Theodore. **Charlie Chaplin.** 1951.

Kahn, Gordon. **Hollywood on Trial.** 1948.

New York Times Film Reviews, 1913-1968. 1970.

Noble, Peter. **Hollywood Scapegoat: The Biography of Erich
    von Stroheim.** 1950.

Robson, E. W. and M. M. **The Film Answers Back.** 1939.

Weinberg, Herman G., editor. **Greed.** 1971.

Wollenberg, H. H. **Anatomy of the Film.** 1947.

Wright, Basil. **The Use of the Film.** 1948.